OMO GHANDI-OLAOYE

Foreword By Dr. Myles Munroe

Silver Spring, Maryland U.S.A

Copyright © By Omo Ghandi-Olaoye

All rights reserved. No portion of this book may be reproduced, stored in a retrieval system, or transmitted in any form, or by any means - electronic, mechanical, photocopy, recording, scanning or other without the written permission of the publisher.

Great Grace Publishing
13132 Shinnecock Drive
Silver Spring, Maryland, 20904 USA

Visit our Website at www.greatgracepublishing.com
Email: info@greatgracepublishing.com

Unless otherwise indicated all Scripture quotations are from the Holy Bible: King James Version (KJV), New International Version, (NIV), New King James Version (NKJV), The Message (MSG) of the Holy Bible. All Rights Reserved

Library of Congress Cataloging-in-Publication Data

I Pray / Omo Ghandi-Olaoye
Includes Illustrations and Photographs
ISBN-10:0-9897908-1-9
ISBN-13: 978-0-9897908-1-9
1. Inspiration – Religious – 1. Title
2013947553

Cover Design & Interior Design by Olawunmi Olafunmiloye

Published in Silver Spring MD by Great Grace .
A registered trademark of Great Grace Publishing LLC.

Printed in the United States of America

I Pray

Table of Contents

INTRODUCTION	17
PRELUDE	24
WHO IS GOD?	29
COME BEFORE GOD WITH PRAISE	31
WHEN YOU NEED FORGIVENESS	37
WHEN YOU ARE AFRAID	43
CANCELLATION OF BAD DREAMS	47
I ADD VALUE	49
FOR PROVISION	51
FOCUS	55
SURROUNDED BY A CLOUD OF WITNESSES	59
WHEN YOU ARE BEING BULLIED	65
CARE-GIVERS	73
WHAT PARTS OF YOUR BODY ARE PRIVATE TO YOU?	75
YOU MUST NEVER BE AFRAID TO REPORT ANY MIS-DEED	78

PROTECT YOUR GATES	79
WISDOM TO MAKE THE RIGHT CHOICES AND TO REJECT DECEIT	81
THE ACADEMIC SCHOOL YEAR	85
FUTURE JOB AND SOURCE OF INCOME	91
FUTURE MARRIAGE	95
I KNOW WHO I AM	101
RESPONSIBILITY	105
THERE IS ONLY ONE GOD	110
SOME OF THE NAMES OF GOD AND THEIR MEANINGS	111
READ YOUR BIBLE AND PRAY	113
THE HOLY SPIRIT	115
THE WORDS: PLEASE, SORRY AND THANK YOU	117
YOUR DRESS CODE	119
BAD HABITS	121
ACCOMPANY YOUR PRAYERS WITH ACTION	127
WITH GOD, NOTHING SHALL BE IMPOSSIBLE	129
GIFTS AND TALENTS	133
ROLE MODELS	137

I Pray

SAFETY	139
OBEDIENCE	141
HOUSEHOLD CHORES	143
RELATIONSHIP WITH GOD	145
CONFIDENCE	147
WISDOM	151
WILLING TO SHARE	153
RELEVANCE	155
RELATIONSHIP WITH MY BROTHERS AND MY SISTERS	157
IDENTIFICATION OF PURPOSE	161
THE ABILITY TO SOLVE PROBLEMS	165
PROTECTION	167
CONTENTMENT	169
CHASTE CONVERSATIONS	171
YOUR BIRTHDAY	177
MY COLLATERAL SECURITY	179
PRAYER AS CONCERNING EVERY MILESTONE IN MY LIFE	183
GOD-CONSCIOUSNESS	187

I Pray

MY PORTIONS	189
CHOICE OF FRIENDS AND ASSOCIATES	191
FAVOR	193
PROMOTION	195
I CAN DO ALL THINGS THROUGH CHRIST	197
SENSE OF DIRECTION	199
THE SPIRIT OF KNOWLEDGE AND UNDERSTANDING	201
BREAK EVERY EVIL FAMILY TREND AND PATTERN	205
WHEN FEELING UNWELL	213
PRAYERS FOR MY FAMILY	219
TO BLESS YOUR FOOD	225
I WILL DO A NEW THING	231

FOREWORD

This exceptional, unique, erudite, eloquent, and immensely thought-provoking work is one of the most important books I have had the privilege to review as it addresses one of the most important issues - PRAYER - but specifically for children.

This work is long overdue and will have a major impact on future generations.

This is an indispensable reading Tool for Parents who want to help and train their Children understand the Principles of Prayer, and how to develop a Prayer life early in life.

This Book lays excellent Biblical Foundations for Effective and Scriptural Prayer and will also benefit Adults who still do not understand the simplicity of Scriptural Prayer.

This is a Profound authoritative work which spans the Wisdom of the ages and yet, breaks new ground in its approach to helping Children pray, and will possibly become a Classic in this and the next Generation.

This exceptional work by Omo Ghandi-Olaoye is one of the most Profound, Practical, Principle-centered approaches to the subject on Prayer for Children I have ever read and I highly recommend this to all Parents and

Sunday schools. The Author's approach to this timely and critical issue of Prayer for Children brings a fresh breath of air that will captivate the heart and the imagination of Children. It will engage their mind while inspiring their spirit.

The Author's ability to leap over complicated theological and metaphysical jargon and reduce complex theories and principles of prayer to simple practical ideas provides the Child with an easy to comprehend Prayer system.

This Work will challenge both Adults and Children alike while embracing the Laymen as it dismantles the mysterious of the Art of Prayer, delivering the Profound in simplicity.

Omo's approach will awaken in the mind of the Child, the untapped inhibiters that retard our Personal Prayer and gives Scriptural Wisdom for a successful Prayer Life.
Omo's sound Scriptural Approach gives a certainty in Prayer that creates a Confidence that makes Prayer easy and a joy.

The Author also integrates into each Chapter, the time-tested Precepts of Scripture, giving each Principle and Subject a practical Application to Life thereby making the entire Process children-friendly.

Every sentence of this Book is pregnant with Wisdom for effective Prayer and I enjoyed the simplicity of using the Word of God in prayer as a powerful and a source of confidence in prayer. This exciting Book will also be used by Adults who for many, prayer is still a challenge. I admonish you to plunge into this ocean of knowledge and watch your children's lives change for the better as you both experience the power of child-like Prayer and Faith.

Dr. Myles Munroe
BFM International
ITWLA
Nassau Bahamas

DEDICATION

Dedicated to my beloved children:
Fehintolu and Toluni

To: The Joyful Mothers' Ministry
To: Every Child born or raised in Jesus House, DC
To: Every Child or Youth who shall use this Book

...Trees of Righteousness, the planting of God
The Heritage of the Lord

The Lord will bless those who bless you
He will show Himself strong and mighty on your behalf
Every Word of God as concerning your lives will manifest in Jesus mighty name
None of it will return to God void
It shall prosper wherein it has been sent
I place upon your lives the Seal of the Living God
The Holy Spirit shall hover over your lives to give it Form and Structure
The Voice of God shall speak Perpetual Light over you.

The Lord of Host is His name
He is your God

.... *I Pray*

Ephesians 3:14-21 *For this cause I bow my knees unto the Father of our Lord Jesus Christ, of whom the whole family in heaven and earth is named. That he would grant you according to the riches of his glory to be strengthened with might by his spirit in the inner man: that Christ may dwell in your hearts by faith; that you, being rooted and grounded in love, may be able to comprehend with all the saints what is the breadth, the length and depth and height and to know the love of Christ which passeth knowledge, that you might be filled with all the fullness of God. Now unto Him that is able to do exceedingly abundantly above all that we ask or think according to the power that worketh in us, unto Him be glory in the church by Christ Jesus throughout all ages, world without end.*

Amen.

Peace

Isaiah 54:13 *And all your children shall be taught of the Lord and great shall be the peace of your children*

INTRODUCTION

Welcome to the place where great and mighty things happen.
It is a place where you can Change things
It is a place where you can Order things.
By "Order" I mean:
A place where you can bring about "Structure"
A place where you can place Orders for your needs and those needs will be met.

It is the place of Prayer

A place of Reverence and Worship
It is a place where we show utmost respect for God
When we come before God, we must know that God is real and that He is a Rewarder of those who seek Him diligently.

One of the ways we seek God is by Prayer
In order for us to be able to pray effectively and also receive answer to our prayers, we must say our prayers based on the Word of God. The Word of God is the Holy Bible.
If You know the Word of God, you will know the mind of God
If You know the mind of God, you will know the Will of God

I Pray...

The Holy Bible is the Will of God
It was written by the inspiration of the Holy Spirit
Everything that we will ever need to know in life and about Life, is in the Bible
Everything that has happened in the past, everything that is happening now, and everything that will happen in the Future is in the Bible.
Every subject and subject matter is in the Bible.
The Answer to every question is in the Bible.
However, some of these things are very deep and you need the help of the Holy Spirit to guide and help you to understand it all very simply and clearly.
That way, you will be able to locate it.
The Holy Spirit is our Teacher.
The Holy Spirit is our Guide
The Holy Spirit is our Helper
He is available to all who seek Him
He is available to help all those who ask Him for Help
He does not discriminate
Remember though:
The Holy Spirit is "Holy"
And so to come before Him, you must turn away from all your evil ways
You must acknowledge all your sins and your evil ways and turn away from them
Your evil ways consist of all your evil thoughts, all your evil words and all your evil deeds
It is important that you acknowledge anything and everything that is evil about you.
You know what those things are.
They are the evil things that you have said
They are the evil thoughts that you think

They are the evil things that you do
They are the evil things that you do in secret and you think nobody saw you
Ask God to forgive you.
God very readily forgives because He loves you so much.
He sent His only begotten Son, Jesus Christ to come and die for your sins.
That He did not spare His Son, shows the extent of God's Love for you.
He will not with-hold any good thing from you
That is how much God cherishes you
Jesus came and died.
But y'see, He did not remain dead, He rose from the dead.
He is the only One who has risen from the dead.
This is because He is also God.
He is God the Son.
He is sitted at the right hand of God the Father and there He lives forever to pray for you and to intercede for you continuously that it may be well with you.
Even at that, He did not leave you without comfort here on earth.
He promised us that when He goes away to take His seat next to God the Father, the Holy Spirit will come
And the Holy Spirit came and He dwells with us
The Holy Spirit not only dwells with us, the Holy Spirit dwells inside of us.

But not everyone has the Holy Spirit.

The Holy Spirit comes by Invitation.
You have to invite Him because He is Holy

But y'see, you cannot invite the Holy Spirit without 1st accepting

I Pray

Jesus Christ as your personal Lord and Savior
This is because, it was because Jesus Christ died and rose that the Holy Spirit came.
You cannot have the Holy Spirit without accepting Jesus Christ – the One who died and rose from the dead
You must accept that this Jesus, is LORD

You cannot accept Jesus Christ without acknowledging God.

All 3 of them are inseparable.
They are called the Holy Trinity.
They are 3-in-One
Undivided
Indivisible.
They walk together and they work together
You need their presence in your life to fervently pray the prayers in this book.
These are the prayers of the Righteous.
The Righteous are the people who work hard to live right according to the Word of God, every day.

The Prayers in this Book are very effective
They are very effectual, and they avail much.
They are very potent and they work wonders.
You will be amazed at the revelations that are in the Bible

You may be asking in your heart:
How do I do all of these things you have mentioned above?
How do I accept Jesus Christ as my personal Lord and Savior?
Just by saying a simple prayer
You can say that Prayer right now.

Pray and say:
Dear Jesus:
I confess that:
You are the Son of God
You are the Word of God
You are my Savior
You are my Redeemer
You came to save me
You died that I might live
You became poor that I might be rich
You were nailed to the cross and you died on the cross that I will not be under any curse
You were smitten, you were beaten up, you were bruised and you were chastised so that I will not be sick, so that I will not be afflicted and so that I will not be in any form of pain or sickness
For all of these that You did for me:
I thank You

I acknowledge all my sins
Sins that I committed in the evil words that I have spoken
Sins that I committed in the evil things I have thought in my heart
Sins that I committed in the evil things that I have done
I remember them all one by one, since the beginning of the Week, the ones I did yesterday, the ones I did since the beginning of today
There are some that I did long ago that I do not remember right now
Dear Lord:
I repent of every one of them
And I ask for Your forgiveness in Jesus mighty name

I start a new life today
I start a new life now

I Pray..

And I start that new life in You.

I am Born again.
Did you just say the above Prayer
Did you mean them from the bottom of your heart?
Wow!

Congratulations.
You are now a Kingdom Citizen.
You are now a Citizen of the Kingdom of God!

Whoa! Whoa!! Whoa!!! Whoa!!!!
Great Benefits accrue to you!
Great Privileges await you!!

Hop on!
Let's ride together!!

....I Pray

PRELUDE

It is important that we pray the Word of God.
The Word of God is the Language of God. The Word of God is the Way of God. The Word of God is the Truth of God.

The Word of God is the Scriptures that have been given to us by the Inspiration of God. The Scriptures contain the Promises of God.

The Promises of God are Treasures.
The Bible says: Ask and it shall be given to you; Knock and it shall be opened to you, Seek and you will find

There is a need for us to Seek what we need and want from the Bible, Knock on God's door of Goodness and Mercy
God will Open.
Enter there in and Ask to make your demands.
He has promised to give you.
God does not fail
God does not lie
Whatever He says He will do, He always does.
That is why it is important that you pray with the Word of God so you will know what God has in store for you, take God's Word back

.... *I Pray*

to Him and pray on it.

Some prayers in this Book will begin with Scriptures.
These Scriptures have been included to enable you know you are praying the Will of God
These Scriptures have also been included so that as you pray frequently with this Book, you will become familiar with the Word of God and as you go on and grow, you will be able to pray the Scriptures and speak the Scriptures naturally from your heart.

Note***
In this Book, there are some words that the 1st letter of that word begins with the Upper case to refer to a Personality. Wherever such words occur, they refer to God the Father, God the Son – Jesus Christ, and God the Holy Spirit.
Words like:
Him
You
Your
He

Scriptures:
Luke 11:1-10
Now it came to pass, as He was praying in a certain place, when He ceased, that one of His disciples said to Him, "Lord, teach us to pray, as John also taught his disciples."
2 So He said to them, "When you pray, say:

Our Father in heaven,
Hallowed be Your name.
Your kingdom come.
Your will be done

I Pray

On earth as it is in heaven.
3 Give us day by day our daily bread.
4 And forgive us our sins,
For we also forgive everyone who is indebted to us.
And do not lead us into temptation,
But deliver us from the evil one."

A Friend Comes at Midnight

5 And He said to them, "Which of you shall have a friend, and go to him at midnight and say to him, 'Friend, lend me three loaves; 6 for a friend of mine has come to me on his journey, and I have nothing to set before him'; 7 and he will answer from within and say, 'Do not trouble me; the door is now shut, and my children are with me in bed; I cannot rise and give to you'? 8 I say to you, though he will not rise and give to him because he is his friend, yet because of his persistence he will rise and give him as many as he needs.
Keep Asking, Seeking, Knocking

9 "So I say to you, ask, and it will be given to you; seek, and you will find; knock, and it will be opened to you. 10 For everyone who asks receives, and he who seeks finds, and to him who knocks it will be opened.
NKJV

Proverbs 3:5-7 *Trust in the LORD with all your heart; and lean not on your own understanding. 6 In all your ways acknowledge Him, and He shall direct your paths. 7 Do not be wise in your own eyes: fear the LORD, and depart from evil.*

Isaiah 30:21 *And your ears shall hear a Word behind you, saying, This is the way, walk you in it, when you turn to the right hand, and when you turn to the left.*

Matthew 21:22 *And all things, what so ever you shall ask in prayer, believing, you shall receive.*

1 John 5:14 *And this is the confidence that we have in Him, that, if we ask any thing according to His Will, He hears us: 15 And if we know that He hears us, what so ever we ask, we know that we have the petitions that we desired of Him.*

WHO IS GOD?

𝕿he bible says: In the beginning, God created the Heavens and the Earth.

God is our Creator and He created the Heavens and the Earth. And much more.

COME BEFORE GOD WITH PRAISE

Pray and say:

My Dear Father in Heaven
I Hallow Your Name
I come before You with all respect to You
You are my Father and You are GOD
I reverence You and I stand in awe of You because You are Holy
Help me to praise You here on earth the way the Angels and the whole heavens praise You every day in heaven
You are the King of Kings
You are the Lord of Lords
You are the Prince of Peace
You are the Lily of the Valley
You are the bright Morning Star
There is no darkness in You
There is no darkness about You
You are so Beautiful
You clothe Yourself with Light
You are the Great Provider
You Provide more than Enough
You are the God who does not sleep

I Pray

You are the God who does not slumber
You watch over me when I am sleeping
You are Deliverer
You are Savior
You are Redeemer
You are Lord of Host
You are the Commander in Chief of the Host of Heaven
Your Army is made up of mighty Angels
These Angels are uncountable
You give them Orders
When You say to them to "Come", they come
When You say to them to "Go" they go
They do whatever You ask them to do and they do it exactly as You tell them to and immediately
You created them to minister to You continually
You created them to minister to You forever and ever
You created them to obey Your Commands

The Angels that Minister before Your Throne have 6 wings
With 2 wings they cover their Faces
With 2 wings they cover their feet
And with 2 wings they fly
They cannot look You in Your Face
This is because they cannot comprehend Your Power and Your Might
In all the greatness of their creation and their make-up and intelligence, they still cannot understand in totality, Your Power and Your Might
You are too much!
Your ways are past finding out
Your Mercies are new every morning
Your Faithfulness is great

I Pray

You move in mysterious ways to perform Your wonders
You walk on the Sea
You ride on the Storm
You are the Greatest God
The Ever-Present God
The Ever-Living God
You are the Father of Light
In You, there is no variableness
In You, there is no shadow of turning
You are Holy
You are full of Glory
And You are full of Honor

When I think of how so great You are
I wonder why you care so much about me
You even assigned Angels to me personally to attend to me and wait on me because I am Your child.
That is the kind of privilege that the children of Rulers and Very Important Personalities have
But You are the King of all kings
You are the Lord of all lords
You are the Ultimate Important
You are Most High
And, I am Your child!

You are the Creator of everything
You created the heavens and the earth
You have made man a little lower than the Angels
Yet You have crowned man with glory and with honor
You love man so much that You sent Your only begotten Son to die that we might all be saved

I Pray

I thank You Lord
I appreciate You Dad!
You are the King of Kings
You are the Lord of Lords
You are Majesty
You Reign forever
You reign in Splendor
Heaven is Your Throne
The whole earth is Your Footstool

Whoooooaa!
What a mighty God You are
Big big God

You are too Great.

The whole Heaven and the whole Earth adore You
All the Angels bow before You
You are Almighty.

.... I Pray

.... *I Pray*

WHEN YOU NEED FORGIVENESS

cripture:

Proverbs 28:13: *He who covers his sins will not prosper; but whoever confesses and forsakes them will have mercy*

Hebrews 4:16: *Let us therefore come boldly unto the throne of grace, that we may obtain mercy and find grace to help in time of need*

Isaiah 1:18
18 "Come now, let us reason together, says the Lord:
though your sins are like scarlet,
they shall be as white as snow;
though they are red like crimson,
they shall become like wool.

Isaiah 59:1-2 *1 Behold, the LORD's hand is not shortened, that it cannot save; neither his ear heavy, that it cannot hear: 2 But your iniquities have separated between you and your God, and your sins have hid his face from you, that he will not hear.*

I Pray

1 John 1:9: *If we confess our sins, he is faithful and just to forgive us our sins, and to cleanse us from all unrighteousness.*

Pray and say:
As I come to You Father
I come boldly before Your Throne of Grace
I come to obtain Mercy
I come to find Grace to help me in the time of my need
I come before Your Most Holy Presence
I remember that Christ shed His blood on the Cross to grant me access
I come pleading the blood of Jesus
I pray that the blood of Jesus that was shed for my sins on the cross of Calvary will grant me access into Your Most Holy presence
I pray that the blood of Jesus will speak for me
I pray that the blood of Jesus will avail for me

I acknowledge every sin in my Life
Every sin of Commission
Every sin of Omission
Every sin that I have committed in the words that I have spoken, in the thoughts of my heart, and in the things that I have done
My sins in my words, my thoughts and my Deeds
The things that I did that I should not have done
The things that I should have done but failed to do
The thoughts that I had in my heart that were not of God
Every spoken word that came from me that God was not pleased with
I repent of them all dear Father
I pray for forgiveness of my sins in all my relationships and my dealings with everyone at home, at School, at Church and everywhere, that did not please God.

.... *I Pray*

I ask for Your forgiveness in the mighty name of Jesus
Dear Lord:
Teach me Your Words
Teach me Your Thoughts
May Your Words become my Words
May Your thoughts become my Thoughts
Help me to be a Reflection of your Character and Your Nature.
The Bible says if any man be in Christ, he is a new Creature.
Old things are passed away and all things become new.

I receive Your forgiveness.
I will not go back to my sins.
I am a brand new person.

I know who I am.
I am the Lord's doing.
I am the Gift of God
I am created to do the right things.
I make rich
I add no sorrow
I am a Child of God
I am created in the image of God
I am created after His likeness

Proverbs 3:5-6
Trust in the Lord with all your heart,
And lean not on your own understanding;
6 In all your ways acknowledge Him,
And He shall direct your paths.
NKJV

I Pray

Pray and Say:
Dear Lord, I trust You with all my heart
You are God and You know all things
I do not depend on anything that I know
I depend on You Lord
As I pray, I invite You
You are my Lord
As I seek You, may I find You
As I knock on Your Door for Mercy, Provision, Help, and everything that I need, kindly open Your door to me
May I have more than enough
As I call on Your Holy Name, please answer me speedily to show up for me and help me
Let me feel Your Presence
Let me know that You are near me
Please speak to me
Let me hear You when You speak to me
Please come down to my level so that I can understand

Dear Father, help me to know Your voice differently from every other voice, in Jesus mighty name I pray. Amen.
As I pray, may my Prayers be followed with answers, and may my Prayers be followed with signs and with wonders in Jesus mighty name.

I pray in the Name of God the Father
I pray in the Name of God the Son
I pray in the Name of God the Holy Spirit
Amen.

.... I Pray

.... *I Pray*

WHEN YOU ARE AFRAID

criptures:

Isaiah54:14 - *In righteousness you shall be established; you shall be far from oppression, for you shall not fear; and from terror, for it shall not come near you. Indeed, they shall surely assemble, but not because of Me, says the Lord; Whoever assembles against you shall fall for your sake.*
Behold, I have created the blacksmith who blows the coals in the fire, who brings forth an instrument for his work; and I have created the spoiler to destroy. No weapon formed against you shall prosper, and every tongue which rises against you in judgment you shall condemn. This is the heritage of the servants of the Lord, and their righteousness is from me, says the Lord.

Isaiah 43:1-3
"Fear not, for I have redeemed you;
I have called you by your name; You are Mine.
2 When you pass through the waters, I will be with you;
And through the rivers, they shall not overflow you.
When you walk through the fire, you shall not be burned,
Nor shall the flame scorch you.

I Pray

3 For I am the Lord your God, The Holy One of Israel, your Savior;
NKJV

1 Corinthians 6:19-20: *Don't you realize that your body is the temple of the Holy Spirit, who lives in you and was given to you by God? You do not belong to yourself, 20 for God bought you with a high price. So you must honor God with your body.*
NLT

Pray and say:
I am the Temple of God and the Holy Spirit lives inside of me

My Foundation is Righteousness
I am established in Righteousness
I am Righteous
I do only the right things
I do only Good
I do not do evil
Evil will always be very far from me
Oppression will be very far from me
Terror will not come near me
I shall not fear
Anyone who comes together against me shall fall for my sake
No weapon formed against me shall succeed
I condemn every tongue that tries to judge me

I am the blessing of God
I make rich
I add no sorrow
I add Value
I do not devalue
I am an Asset

I am not a liability
God will bless those who bless me
God will curse those who curse me
God will fight those who fight me
I am the Heritage of the Lord
All that belongs to God belongs to me
I am the Reward of the Lord
Everything that is a Reward from God manifests in my life
I am a Blessing
I am blessed
I am a Tree of Righteousness
I am the planting of God

In the time of trouble God shall hide me.
God shall hide me in His Pavilion
God shall hide me in the secret place of His tabernacle
God shall set me high upon a rock so that no trouble can come near me
And my head shall be lifted up above my enemies that are around me
They will not have victory over me in Jesus mighty name.

Scripture:

Psalms 27:1-3 *The Lord is my Light and my Salvation; whom shall I fear? The Lord is the strength of my life; of whom shall I be afraid? When the wicked came against me to eat up my flesh, my enemies and foes, they stumbled and fell. Though an army may encamp against me, my heart shall not fear; though war may rise against me, in this I will be confident*

I Pray

Isaiah 41:10 *Fear not, for I am with you; be not dismayed, for I am your God. I will strengthen you, yes, I will help you, for I will uphold you with my righteous right hand*

2 Timothy 1:7 *For God has not given us a spirit of fear, but of power and of love and of a sound mind*

Pray and say:
Help me Lord to trust in You always
Help me Lord to know that You are the God of All Power and that I should not be afraid.

CANCELLATION OF BAD DREAMS

Isaiah 7:7 *Thus says the Lord God: It shall not stand, nor shall it come to pass*

I pray concerning every bad dream I have had; I declare, they shall not stand and they shall not come to pass in Jesus mighty name.

I pray concerning every negative and evil intent and purpose of anyone concerning my life: I declare:
"It will not take place, it will not happen, in the mighty name of Jesus!

Isaiah 54:14-17
In righteousness 1 will be established:
Tyranny will be far from me;
Terror will be far removed from me;
It will not come near me.
The Rod of the wicked shall never rest on my lot
God will frustrate every token of the wicked people concerning me
They will never be able to perform their wicked enterprise as concerning me or as concerning my life

I Pray

The Gates of Hell will never prevail against me in Jesus' mighty name.

Isaiah 49:16 says: *See, I have engraved you on the palm of my hands; your walls are ever before Me.*
May my walls be ever before You Oh Lord, in Jesus mighty name.

I ADD VALUE

I thank You Lord that I can do all that I do for myself I also thank You for the things that I can do for others.

I thank You Lord that:
I can do household chores, I can give myself a bath, and dress myself up nice and good, coordinate my colors and present myself nice and clean, my breath is fresh and my teeth is clean, I have clothes to put on and I have shoes to wear, I clean up after myself
Everywhere around me is nice and tidy
I can make my bed and clean my room and keep my surroundings clean,
I can sort my laundry and do my laundry,
I can clean dishes and keep my surroundings clean
I am obedient at Home and in School
I can run errands for my Mommy and Daddy

Pray and say:
I add value.
I do not devalue
I do only Good.
I do not do evil.

I Pray

Scripture:
Deuteronomy 28:13 *And the Lord shall make you head and not the tail' you shall be above only and not beneath; if you shall hearken unto the commandments of the Lord thy God, which I command you this day, to observe and to do them*

Pray and say:
I am the Head
I am not the tail
I am Above only
I am not beneath
I am 1st
I am not last

The Spirit of God is upon me
The Spirit of Power is upon me
The Spirit of Counsel is upon me
The Spirit of Might is upon me

Dear Lord:
Please continue to be a Dove unto me
Hover over me as the Holy Spirit,
Be a Lion to protect me and to attack all my enemies

....

FOR PROVISION

Scripture:

Psalms 23
The Lord is my shepherd;
I shall not want.
2 He makes me to lie down in green pastures;
He leads me beside the still waters.
3 He restores my soul;
He leads me in the paths of righteousness
For His name's sake.
4 Yea, though I walk through the valley of the shadow of death,
I will fear no evil;
For You are with me;
Your rod and Your staff, they comfort me.
5 You prepare a table before me in the presence of my enemies;
You anoint my head with oil;
My cup runs over.
6 Surely goodness and mercy shall follow me
All the days of my life;
And I will dwell in the house of the Lord, Forever. NKJV
Lord,

I Pray

You are my Shepherd
I shall not lack any good thing
May my pastures always be Green and Fresh
Lead me beside Still Waters
May my Waters not be troubled

Restore my soul
Lead me in the path of Righteousness because I bear Your name
May I always be at the right place at the right time
May I do only good
May evil be far from me
May your Rod and your Staff comfort me continually

Dear Lord, prepare a table before me severally every day:
A Table of Goodness, Mercy, Peace, Joy, Greatness, Promotion, Excellent Health, Wealth, Knowledge, Understanding, Wisdom, and all the good things that I need everyday till I become very old

Dear Father, please give me good food to eat, good clothes to wear, great education, and a beautiful home to live in

Dear Lord, before my need arises, may my supplies be waiting in Jesus mighty name.
Dear Lord, anoint my head with oil
Anoint my head with the oil of Gladness, of Favor
May Your Goodness and Your Mercy follow me all the days of my Life
May I dwell in Your presence every day

.... I Pray

FOCUS

cripture:

Proverbs 22:6
Train up a child in the way he should go,
And when he is old he will not depart from it.
NKJV

Pray and say:
Dear Lord, do not let cigarettes, drugs, and strong drinks ever come near me in Jesus mighty name
Do not let me smoke cigarettes or drink alcohol or any strong drink
May I never do drugs
May the choices that I make be good
May the choices that I make be of God
May the choices that I make be right
May the choices that I make be wise
Give me wisdom to make godly choices in the friends that that I make and in the company that I keep
May my associations and the friends that I make and the friends that I keep have a godly orientation, may they have a godly foundation and may they be friends that do the right things, wear the right

I Pray ....

things, go to the right places, and keep the precepts and the mandate of God
Please Father, give me the ability to know what is good and what is evil.

May I never be mistaken or confused or misled about my Creation and my Gender
May nobody ever be able to convince me about ways that are against the Word of God
I pray for the Wisdom to be able to tell good from evil
I pray for the boldness to be able to always choose good over evil in Jesus mighty name.

....*I Pray*

SURROUNDED BY A CLOUD OF WITNESSES

cripture:

Hebrews 12:1-2
Therefore we also, since we are surrounded by so great a cloud of witnesses, let us lay aside every weight, and the sin which so easily ensnares us, and let us run with endurance the race that is set before us, 2 looking unto Jesus, the author and finisher of our faith, who for the joy that was set before Him endured the cross, despising the shame, and has sat down at the right hand of the throne of God.
NKJV

There are different kinds of Witnesses

There are examples of the Witnesses of those who are in Ivory Towers and in College studying to graduate and get a Degree in order to get great jobs
There are the Witnesses of those who are on Wall Street
There are the Witnesses of those who are in Church
There are the Witnesses of those who end up well in Life
They have great Jobs
They have great and beautiful Homes

I Pray

They own great Cars
They go on fun-filled Vacations to great places
They fly the best of Classes on the Airplanes
They provide for themselves and their Families
They are Very Important Personalities

Pray and say:
Dear Lord, may I be like the people described above in Jesus mighty name.
Help me to study and read my books to show myself approved for promotion in my Life
Help me to do the right things that will enable me earn the right rewards that are described above in Jesus mighty name.

There are also some other kinds of Witnesses.

There are the Witnesses of those who are in Jail
There are the Witnesses of those who are on the Streets begging
There are the Witnesses of those who fight on the Streets
They fight with knives and guns and they carry all kinds of weapons
They take people's stuff from them by force
They bully others
They do not take turns
They take advantage of other people
There are the Witnesses of those who never end up well in life. They always end up in jail and spend the rest of their lives in jail.
They cannot work and they cannot earn good money and so they cannot live a good life or provide a good life for their children and their Spouses.
They cannot contribute to or impact the Society positively.
There are the Witnesses of those who are Homeless

There are the Witnesses of those who cannot buy themselves their own clothes and pay for them
They are the Witnesses of those who permanently have to wait on others to give to them before they can have
There are the Witnesses of those who are in Mad People's Homes because they did drugs
There are the Witnesses of those who are permanently Jobless
There are the Witnesses of those who are not doing well at all and they are struggling and suffering

Pray and say:
Dear Lord, may I never be like the people described above in Jesus mighty name.
May I always listen to good Counsel
May I always listen to the uncompromising Word of God
May I do the things that will keep me far away from the things described above in Jesus mighty name
May I be hardworking
Help me to take my education and my good manners seriously
May I be respectful to others
May I respect other people's feelings
May I respect other people's property
Help me to find favor that will promote me and beautify my life in Jesus mighty name
May I serve God all of my life
May I be God's friend
May God be my friend too
In Jesus mighty name I pray. Amen.

Abraham was God's friend and God always told Abraham everything He wanted to do so that Abraham can pray and talk to God about it
May I also be God's friend too and may God also always tell me stuff

I Pray..

so that I too can pray to God about them
God told Abraham where to go. He told Abraham to leave his Country and go to a place God told him to go and Abraham obeyed

Pray and say:
May I always obey God.
May I be obedient to my Parents
May I obey those God has put in authority over me
May I obey my Teachers
May I obey the Law

God told Abraham not to take Lot his nephew and Abraham disobeyed.

Pray and say:
May I never disobey God
God told Abraham He was going to destroy the people that lived in Sodom and Gomorrah because they were committing sin. Abraham was living with these people. God told Abraham to leave these people so that he will not be destroyed with them. Abraham listened to God and obeyed God and so Abraham left with his Family and they were saved because they listened to God and obeyed God.

Pray and say:
May I always listen to God, May I always obey God, and may I be saved from destruction in Jesus mighty name.

....I Pray

....

WHEN YOU ARE BEING BULLIED

Scripture:

1 Samuel 17:1-51
Now the Philistines gathered together their armies to battle; and they were gathered together at Socoh, which belongeth to Judah, and encamped between Socoh and Azekah, in Ephes-dammim.
2 And Saul and the men of Israel were gathered together, and encamped in the vale of Elah, and set the battle in array against the Philistines.
3 And the Philistines stood on the mountain on the one side, and Israel stood on the mountain on the other side: and there was a valley between them.
4 And there went out a champion out of the camp of the Philistines, named Goliath, of Gath, whose height was six cubits and a span.
5 And he had a helmet of brass upon his head, and he was clad with a coat of mail; and the weight of the coat was five thousand shekels of brass.
6 And he had greaves of brass upon his legs, and a javelin of brass between his shoulders.
7 And the staff of his spear was like a weaver's beam; and his spear's head (weighed) six hundred shekels of iron: and his shield-bearer

I Pray

went before him.

8 And he stood and cried unto the armies of Israel, and said unto them, Why are ye come out to set your battle in array? am not I a Philistine, and ye servants to Saul? choose you a man for you, and let him come down to me.

9 If he be able to fight with me, and kill me, then will we be your servants; but if I prevail against him, and kill him, then shall ye be our servants, and serve us.

10 And the Philistine said, I defy the armies of Israel this day; give me a man, that we may fight together.

11 And when Saul and all Israel heard those words of the Philistine, they were dismayed, and greatly afraid.

12 Now David was the son of that Ephrathite of Beth-lehem-judah, whose name was Jesse; and he had eight sons: and the man was an old man in the days of Saul, stricken (in years) among men.

13 And the three eldest sons of Jesse had gone after Saul to the battle: and the names of his three sons that went to the battle were Eliab the first-born, and next unto him Abinadab, and the third Shammah.

14 And David was the youngest; and the three eldest followed Saul.

15 Now David went to and fro from Saul to feed his father's sheep at Beth-lehem.

16 And the Philistine drew near morning and evening, and presented himself forty days.

17 And Jesse said unto David his son, Take now for thy brethren an ephah of this parched grain, and these ten loaves, and carry (them) quickly to the camp to thy brethren;

20 And David rose up early in the morning, and left the sheep with a keeper, and took, and went, as Jesse had commanded him; and he came to the place of the wagons, as the host which was going forth to the fight shouted for the battle.

22 And David left his baggage in the hand of the keeper of the baggage, and ran to the army, and came and saluted his brethren.

23 And as he talked with them, behold, there came up the champion, the Philistine of Gath, Goliath by name, out of the ranks of the Philistines, and spake according to the same words: and David heard them.
24 And all the men of Israel, when they saw the man, fled from him, and were sore afraid.
32 And David said to Saul, Let no man's heart fail because of him; thy servant will go and fight with this Philistine.
33 And Saul said to David, Thou art not able to go against this Philistine to fight with him; for thou art but a youth, and he a man of war from his youth.
34 And David said unto Saul, Thy servant was keeping his father's sheep; and when there came a lion, or a bear, and took a lamb out of the flock,
35 I went out after him, and smote him, and delivered it out of his mouth; and when he arose against me, I caught him by his beard, and smote him, and slew him.
36 Thy servant smote both the lion and the bear: and this uncircumcised Philistine shall be as one of them, seeing he hath defied the armies of the living God.
37 And David said, Jehovah that delivered me out of the paw of the lion, and out of the paw of the bear, he will deliver me out of the hand of this Philistine. And Saul said unto David, Go, and Jehovah shall be with thee.
38 And Saul clad David with his apparel, and he put a helmet of brass upon his head, and he clad him with a coat of mail.
39 And David girded his sword upon his apparel, and he assayed to go; for he had not proved it. And David said unto Saul, I cannot go with these; for I have not proved them. And David put them off him.
40 And he took his staff in his hand, and chose him five smooth stones out of the brook, and put them in the shepherd's bag which he had, even in his wallet; and his sling was in his hand: and he drew

I Pray ....

near to the Philistine.

41 And the Philistine came on and drew near unto David; and the man that bare the shield went before him.

42 And when the Philistine looked about, and saw David, he disdained him; for he was but a youth, and ruddy, and withal of a fair countenance.

43 And the Philistine said unto David, Am I a dog, that thou comest to me with staves? And the Philistine cursed David by his gods.

44 And the Philistine said to David, Come to me, and I will give thy flesh unto the birds of the heavens, and to the beasts of the field.

45 Then said David to the Philistine, Thou comest to me with a sword, and with a spear, and with a javelin: but I come to thee in the name of Jehovah of hosts, the God of the armies of Israel, whom thou hast defied.

46 This day will Jehovah deliver thee into my hand; and I will smite thee, and take thy head from off thee; and I will give the dead bodies of the host of the Philistines this day unto the birds of the heavens, and to the wild beasts of the earth; that all the earth may know that there is a God in Israel,

47 and that all this assembly may know that Jehovah saveth not with sword and spear: for the battle is Jehovah's, and he will give you into our hand.

48 And it came to pass, when the Philistine arose, and came and drew nigh to meet David, that David hastened, and ran toward the army to meet the Philistine.

49 And David put his hand in his bag, and took thence a stone, and slang it, and smote the Philistine in his forehead; and the stone sank into his forehead, and he fell upon his face to the earth.

50 So David prevailed over the Philistine with a sling and with a stone, and smote the Philistine, and slew him; but there was no sword in the hand of David.

51 Then David ran, and stood over the Philistine, and took his sword,

and drew it out of the sheath thereof, and slew him, and cut off his head therewith. And when the Philistines saw that their champion was dead, they fled.
ASV

Scripture:
1 Thessalonians 5:22: *Abstain from all appearance of evil*

James 4:7: *Resist the devil (stand firm against him), and he will flee from you.*
Joshua 1:9: *Yes, be bold and strong! Banish fear and doubt! For remember, the Lord your God is with you wherever you go.*

Philemon 8: *For this reason I could be bold enough, as your brother in Christ, to order you to do what should be done*

Romans 15:18: *I will be bold and speak only about what Christ has done through me to lead the Gentiles to obey God. He has done this by means of words and deeds.*

2 Corinthians 10:2: *But I beg you that when I am present I may not be bold with that confidence by which I intend to be bold against some, who think of us as if we walked according to the flesh. For though we walk in the flesh, we do not war according to the flesh. For the weapons of our warfare are not carnal but mighty in God for pulling down strongholds, casting down arguments and every high thing that exalts itself against the knowledge of God, bringing every thought into captivity to the obedience of Christ, and being ready to punish all disobedience when your obedience is fulfilled.*

Colossians 2:15: *Having disarmed principalities and powers, He made a public spectacle of them, triumphing over them in it*

I Pray

Luke 18:7-8: *And shall not God avenge His elect, that cry to Him day and night, and (yet) He is longsuffering over them? I say unto you, that He will avenge them speedily.*

Pray and say:
Dear Jesus:
Strengthen me and anoint me afresh
May I not be distracted
Please help me remain focused.
Cleanse me from everything that contaminates me
Cleanse me from anything that contaminates me.
Give me the Spirit of Boldness
Take the Spirit of Fear away from me
May I be bold enough to report every mis-deed to those who have been put in authority over me in School, at Home, in Church, at Play and everywhere I find myself
I will not be timid
I will not be fearful
I will not be afraid of those who rise up to intimidate me and bully me
I will be quick to take note of their evil intentions
I will not be silent
I will not condone it
I will rise up to their evil intent
I will stand up to their misdeeds
I will make a report of it to my Parents
I will make a report of them to my Teachers
I will make a report of them to the Head of School
I will make a report of them to the Police
I will make sure the necessary action is taken to ensure that I am not threatened or made to feel uncomfortable in School, at Work and at Play

.... *I Pray*

I will not be placed in any position or form of danger
I will make a show of it openly
I will not be silent until it is addressed
My Confidence will not be messed up
I will be of good behavior
I will keep good company
I will be quick to stand up to evil
I will resist the devil and make sure he flees from me
I will flee every appearance of evil in Jesus mighty name
I am a Child of Light
Make me a Vessel unto Honor

PRAYERS FOR MY CARE-GIVERS

May I always listen to all those that God has put in authority over me to guide me
May they guide me unto all truth
May they not deceive me.
May they not lead me astray.
May they not make me disobey God.
May they not make me disobey the Laws of the Land.
May they not take undue advantage of me
May they add only value to my life and not devalue me
May they not take advantage of my innocence
May they not manipulate me and my ways and my thoughts

Help me Lord to flee every appearance of evil
Help me to always be conscious of my surroundings
May I always be at the right place at the right time.

Pray and say:
I pray for my Mom, I pray for my Dad, I pray for my Teachers at School, I pray for my Teachers in Church, I pray for my Care-givers.

I Pray

Dear Holy Spirit, teach them and guide them as they take care of me.
When they are not around me, please watch their backs as concerning me.
Keep me from evil always.

Give me plenty of Wisdom dear Jesus.
I pray dear Lord that You will always take control of the thoughts of my Caregivers
Dear Jesus, may it be impossible for evil to penetrate me
May I never be deceived.
I pray Lord that in my time of vulnerability, Lord, You will show up for me to save me and deliver me.

WHAT PARTS OF YOUR BODY ARE PRIVATE TO YOU?

Your chest area (that is, your breasts), your bottom or your butts, your under arm, in between your thighs, you must not let anyone breathe into your ears, they cannot touch your breasts or play with your breasts, they cannot come between your thighs or run their hands in between your thighs, they cannot tickle you, they cannot sit you on their laps, they cannot press their bodies against your body, you cannot lay on the same bed with the opposite sex or gender not even as Teenagers.

Check out the kind of look grown-ups give to you

Do they wink at you?

Check out their glances especially when no one else is watching

Do they try to come unnecessarily close to you and try to touch you with their body?

Never be left alone in their company

Beware of such Uncles, Cousins, Family Friends, Pastors, Church Members, Domestic Staff, anyone who serves Dad and Mom by reason of their jobs or who help out in one way or the other that you might tend to trust

No welcome and goodbye hugs. No welcome and goodbye kisses.

You have no business with such pleasantries

Some people who are the same gender as you are just as dangerous as the opposite sex. So stay away from anyone who makes any attempt to touch the parts of your body that are private to you.

You must never let anyone touch you in places that are private to you.

You must never let any man or woman touch you in places that are private to you.

Godly Mom and Dad are an exception to this rule.

Where a Dad or Step-Dad, or Mom's boyfriend tries to touch any of the parts of your body that are private to you, make an instant report of it to your Mom's Sister that you trust, or to your Pastor's wife.
Confide in them and they will shield and find ways of protecting you from abuse.

Medical Doctors can examine you, and when they do, there must be somebody else with you when the Doctor is examining you.
No one should tickle you.

If anyone tries to touch you in your private areas, you must speak out at the scene and make it public
You must always tell it to Mom and Dad and you must do so immediately.
You must never be afraid to tell.
And you must never be afraid to shout.
You must never think Mommy and Daddy will be mad at you for telling.

A Grandma who had a Doctor's appointment once entrusted the care of her grandchild to an old man her age who was her neighbor and with whom they attended the same Church.

Granmda left her grandchild with this old man for a couple of hours to enable her go for her Doctor's visit.

While she was away, this old man sexually abused that little 8 year old girl. He threatened her that if she told her Grandma a word about it, he would kill her Grandma.

He scared her so much by what he said that she was afraid to tell. Grandma was all she had as both her parents were divorced and her Grandma had taken her away from her Mom in order for her Mom to get back on her feet after the painful divorce. She did not even know where her Mom was or have any details.

She feared that if the old man killed her Grandma, she will be thrown out into the streets with no one. And so she kept quite. And severally, Grandma will leave her with the old man whenever she had to go out because she trusted the old man because she felt he was old enough to be her grand dad and also because he was in Church with her and thought he was a good Christian.

I Pray...

YOU MUST NEVER BE AFRAID TO REPORT ANY MIS-DEED

I want to let you know never to be afraid to tell of any mis-deed. Never be afraid to report any abuse.
You must never be afraid of their threats.
You must tell it immediately to Mom, Dad, Grandma, Grandpa, your Teacher at School or to the Police

You must never be afraid of their threat to kill anyone around you. You must also never be afraid of how Mom and Dad will react towards you if you tell it to them
God put Mom and Dad there to protect you

(**Colossians 2:14-15:** *Having wiped out the handwriting of requirements that was against us, which was contrary to us. And He has taken it out of the way, having nailed it to the cross. Having disarmed principalities and powers, He made a public spectacle of them, triumphing over them in it*).

PROTECT YOUR GATES

Your Gates are your eyes, your ears, your heart.

You must be very careful and mindful of the kind of Books you read, or the kind of Movies you watch or the Channels you watch on TV or the Sites you surf on the Internet and Youtube

The bible says:
Whatsoever things are pure, whatsoever things are lovely, whatsoever things are of good report, if there be any virtue, and if there be any praise, think on these things – **Philippians 4:8**

Be careful what you watch on TV and on Youtube. As children, you do not have any business with some of these things.
Be careful the kind of friends you keep and play with.
When they use bad words and want to make you do bad stuff, tell on them to Mommy, Daddy, or your Teacher and keep away from them.
Do not be friends with them.
It is okay not to be their friend!

PRAYER FOR WISDOM TO MAKE THE RIGHT CHOICES AND TO REJECT DECEIT

Solomon when he was 13 years old, he became a King.
God asked Solomon what Solomon wants God to give to him.
Solomon did not ask for a 3 DS, or an I-Touch, an I-pad, a Chrome Book, the latest Computer Game, the latest Computer Technology, or a Puppy, or a Toy.
Solomon asked God to give him Wisdom.
This is because he knew if God gives him Wisdom, with that Wisdom, he will be able to get anything and everything that he will ever want or need. He will be able to get a 3DS, an I-Touch, an I-Phone, an I-pad, a Chrome Book, whatever new Technology comes out, a Puppy, and much more.
We must pray to God to give us the Wisdom to always ask for the right things.
We must pray to God to give us the Wisdom to always ask for the right things and make the right choices in life.

There are things that money can buy.
There are also things that money cannot buy.
The things that money cannot buy will always give us the Wealth to buy the things that money can buy.
So, we must always ask God for Wisdom to know what to ask for

I Pray

every time and what to do every time and in every situation.

We must ask God for the Wisdom to choose our friends, right associations, and keep good company.
Some people will come around us to tempt us and to try to deceive us to do the wrong things.
They know who your Dad and Mom are
They know you go to Church and that you are being brought up in the way of God to be great in life
They do not want you to be great
They will want to deceive you to ask your Dad and Mom for money to do the wrong things or even to take things without permission because they know you have those things at home
Satan tempted Jesus too in the wilderness and tried to make Jesus do the wrong things

Scripture:
Matthew 4:1-11
Satan tempted Jesus and wanted Jesus to turn stones to bread
He wanted Jesus to jump from a high place down so He can hurt Himself
Satan even quoted the bible wrongly to use it to deceive Jesus to do the wrong thing
But Jesus knew who He was
Nobody could define Jesus to Jesus
He knew Himself for Himself
He was confident
Jesus knew the things that He can do and the right time to do those things
Jesus knew the things that were being told Him were not from God and so He chased Satan away by always giving Satan the right answer from the Word of God.

A lot of people and a lot of things represent Satan.
There are some people who are a part of our lives and the things they try to tell us and the kind of counsel they give to us continually are meant to deceive us and lead us astray and not do us any good
There are also a lot of things out there that are available for us to buy or own, or watch, or see.
On the surface, they look beautiful and harmless, but substantially, in contents and in value, they do us no good.

Pray and say:
Dear Lord, I pray for Wisdom.
I pray for Wisdom to be able to know what is good from what is bad
I pray for Wisdom to be able to know what is right from what is wrong
I Pray for Wisdom to be able to always choose right and not choose wrong
I pray for Wisdom to always choose what is good and never choose what is bad

May I have the boldness to always do so and never be afraid or ashamed of anybody or anything when I do so in Jesus mighty name.

May I never be ashamed of what my friends will think or say about me
May I never be afraid of what my friends will say or think about me
May I be bold to always do the right thing and to look my friends in the face
May I never be afraid of friends who try to bully
Give me the boldness and the courage to always stand up to them by bringing attention to them and to make a report of their ways.

THE ACADEMIC SCHOOL YEAR

Scripture:

Daniel 6:3 *Then this Daniel was preferred above the presidents and princes, because an excellent spirit was in him, and the king thought to set him over the whole realm*

Pray and say:
I pray that an excellent spirit will be upon me
I pray that I will find favor with all those in Authority in whatever situations I find myself in and in whatever place I am in
I pray that I will find favor always

I pray that much will be entrusted into my care
I pray that I will be dependable, responsible, accountable, reliable, resourceful, creative, greatly endowed and Trustworthy, in the mighty name of Jesus.
I pray against the spirit of mediocrity
I will not be a Mediocre in Jesus mighty name.
I pray against every evil tongue of people who try to speak and make me feel I am less of God than I really am
I condemn every such tongue in Jesus' mighty name

I Pray

I reject them and I cancel their utterances with the blood of Jesus;
I am more than a Conqueror through Christ who strengthens me.

I commit the times and the seasons of my Life into the hands of the Almighty God
I pray that God will show me mercy
May God's goodness and mercy follow me continually
I pray the Holy Spirit of God will be unto me a Pillar of Cloud to guide me during the day and a Pillar of Fire to guide me at Night
I commit my School Year into the hands of God
I commit my going out and my coming in
And my sleeping and my waking into the hands of God

I commit my learning and my understanding, and my remembrance of the things that I have been taught into the hands of God
I commit my Grades, my Credits hours, and my Internships into the hands of God
I commit my needs, my Tuition, my School Supplies, my Uniforms, my Transportation, my Accommodation, and my provisions for the whole of this year and for my lifetime, into the hands of the Lord
I commit my studies, my exams, my promotions, my interviews, my employments, my relationships, my choice of friends, my future in my choice of a life Partner, my marriage, my childbearing and my children.
I commit everything that pertains to my living a fulfilled life into the hands of God

I pray concerning the seasons of my whole life at this moment in Jesus mighty name
Dear Lord: May it be well with me all the days of my life in Jesus mighty name.

Pray and Say:
May I have the understanding of Daniel.
Daniel had an Excellent Spirit.
May I understand everything that my Teacher teaches me.
Make it easy for me
Help my Teacher to speak and teach in the way that I can understand
Grant my Teacher Patience
Give my teacher the right words and the easy words to explain what is being taught so that I can always understand
Help me Lord to enjoy my Teacher's teaching
May I never be distracted
May I enjoy learning and knowledge

I pray for Retentive Memory
Dear Lord, help me to always remember everything I am taught in School and how they have been taught me.
Help me Lord to be well behaved in Class
Help me Lord to concentrate in Class when my teacher is teaching
Help me Lord not to be distracted with the goings on with my other friends
Help me Lord not to be carried away in my thoughts when my Teacher is teaching.

May I never forget what I am taught
May I never forget how I have been taught
Give me the boldness to speak up to let my Teacher know what I do not understand
Give my Teacher the grace and the patience to come to my level to teach me, make it easy for me and help me understand
As I remember Lord, please help me to always express it in my speaking and in my writing and even in my actions.

I Pray

I pray for a good sense of judgment in applying what I have been taught in class to when I am answering the questions in my exams. Give me the wisdom to understand exam questions and to answer them correctly
I also pray for speed under exam conditions
May I start my exams at the time I am supposed to begin.
May I end at the stipulated time I have been given to finish.
May I have answered all the questions I have been required to answer within the stipulated time that I am given for my Exam.

May I be on Honor Roll
May I always use my best manners and be of good behavior in School and at all times
May I always listen to my Teacher and obey my Teacher
May I be a disciplined child
May I graduate from Elementary School to Middle School
May I graduate from Middle School to High School
May I graduate to College
I pray that I will graduate well from College
I pray that I will do a Master's Degree
I pray that I will do a Doctorate Degree

.... I Pray

FUTURE JOB AND SOURCE OF INCOME

I pray concerning my choice of a Job or my source of income in the future.

Scripture:
The Earth is the Lord's and the fullness thereof
The Silver and the Gold
The Cattle upon a thousand hills belong unto our God
God grants us the desires of our hearts according to His riches in Glory by Christ Jesus
The Hearts of Kings are in the hands of the Lord and like the rivers of water He turns it whichever way He chooses

Pray and say:
Dear Lord: Network me with people who can Help me and promote me
Showcase me
Surround me with favor like a Shield

The Laborer is worthy of his hire

I Pray

As I get out of College, I pray for wisdom for the choice of a Source of Income

I pray for Strength to do the work and accommodate the responsibilities that come with my position

I pray for the Favor that brings Promotion

I pray for maturity

I pray for wisdom and the temperament required for the challenges that are associated with the job

I pray Lord for excellent health to enjoy Your blessings in my Life.

I pray for a source of income that can take care of my bills and leave me with extra to leave a comfortable life –

I pray for an Income that will enable me own a car, own a home, go on vacations, and prepare for marriage, be comfortably married, take care of my children and still have enough to save.

I pray for a good sense of judgment in applying what I have been taught in class to when I am answering the questions in my exams. Give me the wisdom to understand exam questions and to answer them correctly

I also pray for speed under exam conditions

May I start my exams at the time I am supposed to begin.

May I end at the stipulated time I have been given to finish.

May I have answered all the questions I have been required to answer within the stipulated time that I am given for my Exam.

Scripture:
John 6:9-13

9 There is a boy here that hath five barley loaves, and two fishes; but what are these among so many?
10 Then Jesus said: Make the men sit down. Now there was much grass in the place. The men therefore sat down, in number about five thousand.
11 And Jesus took the loaves: and when he had given thanks, he distributed to them that were set down. In like manner also of the fishes, as much as they would.
12 And when they were filled, he said to his disciples: Gather up the fragments that remain, lest they be lost.
13 They gathered up therefore, and filled twelve baskets with the fragments of the five barley loaves, which remained over and above to them that had eaten.
NKJV

Pray and say:
I pray Lord that you will bless whatever I own and make it more than enough for me.
I pray dear Lord that I will always have more than enough to meet my needs in Jesus mighty name.

FUTURE MARRIAGE

I pray concerning my Relationships as I work towards Marriage.
Help me Lord to face my studies and complete my College education and have a good job before I begin to consider Marriage.

May I not be involved in immoral things that cause people to have children before they get married.

The Story of Adam and Eve

Scripture:

Genesis 2:20-24
20 And the man gave names to all cattle, and to the birds of the heavens, and to every beast of the field; but for man there was not found a help meet for him.
21 And Jehovah God caused a deep sleep to fall upon the man, and he slept; and he took one of his ribs, and closed up the flesh instead thereof:
22 and the rib, which Jehovah God had taken from the man, made he a woman, and brought her unto the man.

I Pray

23 And the man said, This is now bone of my bones, and flesh of my flesh: she shall be called Woman, because she was taken out of Man.

24 Therefore shall a man leave his father and his mother, and shall cleave unto his wife: and they shall be one flesh.
ASV

Pray and say:
God created Adam.
And out of the ribs of Adam, God created Eve.
God brought Eve to Adam.
Eve did not know any other man before Adam.
It was through Adam and by Adam, that Eve had all her children.
Adam was the 1st and only man that Eve slept with.
And it was through Adam and by Adam that she became pregnant and had Cain and Abel.

This tells me Lord that this is Your intention for me.
If You wanted it otherwise, You would have created several Eves for Adam or created several Adams for Eve or created another Adam for Adam or another Eve for Eve
But Lord You created them male and Female and You wanted One man for One Woman only.

Pray and say:
Order my Life dear Lord.
May there be order and structure in my Life.
Help me to keep my Virtues intact.
Help me to maintain my Virginity
Help me to live and maintain a Lifestyle that will enable me keep my Virginity until I get married.
Please Lord, may I not live a lifestyle that will make me begin to

bear children before Marriage.
May I not live a perverse lifestyle in the mighty name of Jesus.
May I not live a lifestyle that will make me ashamed
May I not live a lifestyle that will become a stigma to me
May I not live a lifestyle where I will be looked down upon
May I not live a lifestyle that I cannot afford
May I not live a lifestyle where I cannot take care of my children and my responsibilities by myself
May I not live a lifestyle where I will depend on other people to take up my responsibilities for me
In Jesus' mighty name.

Pray and say:
When I am done with College, I pray that I will make the right choice of who to marry and spend the rest of my life with.
I pray Lord that I will be attracted to someone who is a true child of God
I pray Lord that I will be attracted to someone who has the fear of God
I pray that I will be attracted to someone who is disciplined and has self control
I pray I will be attracted to someone who tells the Truth and will not deceive me or lead me astray
I pray I will be attracted to someone who truly loves me
I pray I will be attracted to someone who has the ability to take care of me
I pray I will be attracted to someone who will take care of me
I pray I will be attracted to someone who will support me
I pray I will be attracted to someone who has a great heart
I pray I will be married to someone who is selfless towards me
I pray I will be attracted to someone who is genuine
I pray I will be attracted to someone who is compassionate

I Pray

I pray Lord that I will be married to someone who is not contentious

I pray that I will be married to someone who is peaceful and loves peace

Someone who has the same godly and academic Values that I stand upon

I pray I will be married to someone who will not devalue me

I pray I will be married to someone who will not reduce me

I pray I will be married to someone who will not make me small

I pray I will be married to someone who will not make me few

I pray I will be married to someone who will add value to my life

I pray I will be married to someone who will not forsake me

I pray I will be married to someone who will be my friend and my confidant

I pray I will be married to someone who is Wise

I pray I will be attracted only to someone whose blood group compatible with mine

I pray Lord that my marriage will not bring me sorrow

I pray that I will be married to that Someone who completes me

In Jesus mighty name. Amen.

.... I Pray

I KNOW WHO I AM

cripture:

Psalms 23:5-6
5 You prepare a table before me in the presence of my enemies;
You anoint my head with oil;
My cup runs over.
6 Surely goodness and mercy shall follow me
All the days of my life;
And I will dwell in the house of the Lord
Forever.
NKJV

Genesis 22:17 *That in blessing I will bless you, and in multiplying I will multiply your seed as the stars of heaven, and as the sand which is upon the seashore, and your seed shall possess the gate of his enemies*

Pray and Say:
I draw the bloodline of Jesus between me and the works of Darkness.

I Pray

I commit my names to God
My names shall never be heard in jail houses
When it is time for me to begin Courtship, it will be holy and it will be divine; it will be testimonial; it will be real; I will not be jilted, disappointed, or be a victim of heartbreak
I shall be very well married
I shall have a good source of income
I shall have a great job
The Lord will bless the works of my hands
I shall always be relevant
The Spirit of Preference is upon me.
I shall always be preferred for favor.

Abraham was great
Isaac was very great
Jacob was exceedingly great

I shall be greater than my Parents

I shall be fruitful in male and in female children
I shall see my children's children
The privileges that my Parents missed or never had, shall abound unto me
Much more privileges shall abound unto me
I shall be full of grace

I shall have a wonderful relationship with my Dad and Mom
I will not cause my Parents any anxieties
I shall have wonderful relationships with my children
I shall understand them, and they shall understand me

There shall be love and a binding in our home

I Pray

I am not brought forth for trouble
I will not bring forth for trouble
I cause no grief
I cause no sorrow
I cause no pain
I pray for Promotion
Promotion in my studies and in my Grades
Promotion from one level of my Life to another
My coasts shall be enlarged
I shall discover my potentials
I shall maximize my potentials
I shall go above and I shall go beyond my circumstances
The Spirit of Excellence is upon me
The Spirit of Preference is upon me
The Spirit of Solution is upon me
Through God and by God, I have the Wisdom and the ability to resolve every problem that comes before me
No Problem has the ability to overcome me because I am a child of God
I shall possess the gates of my enemies
I am Head and I am not tail
I am above only and I am not last
I am above only and I am not beneath

I Pray

RESPONSIBILITY

The bible says: In the beginning, God created the Heavens and the Earth
God is our Creator and He created the Heavens and the Earth
God created every one of us to be either male or Female, boys and girls, man and woman.
And so God created our Daddies to be men and our Mommies to be women.
God did not create another man for Adam and God did not create another woman for Eve. Relationships such as these displease God and that was why God destroyed and killed all the people in Sodom and Gomorrah. This is a sin and an abomination. God hates it and God can destroy and kill people because of this sin.

Scripture
Genesis 19:1-23
2 And he said, Behold now, my lords, turn aside, I pray you, into your servant's house, and tarry all night, and wash your feet, and ye shall rise up early, and go on your way. And they said, Nay. But we will abide in the street all night.
3 And he urged them greatly. And they turned in unto him, and entered into his house. And he made them a feast, and did bake

I Pray

unleavened bread, and they did eat.
4 But before they lay down, the men of the city, (even) the men of Sodom, compassed the house round, both young and old, all the people from every quarter.
5 And they called unto Lot, and said unto him, Where are the men that came in to thee this night? Bring them out unto us, that we may know them.
6 And Lot went out unto them to the door, and shut the door after him.
7 And he said, I pray you, my brethren, do not so wickedly.
9 And they said, Stand back. And they said, This one fellow came in to sojourn, and he will needs be a judge. Now will we deal worse with thee, than with them. And they pressed sore upon the man, even Lot, and drew near to break the door.
10 But the Angels put forth their hand, and brought Lot into the house to them, and shut to the door.
11 And the Angels smote the men that were at the door of the house with blindness, both small and great, so that they wearied themselves to find the door.
12 And the Angels said unto Lot, Hast thou here any besides? Son-in-law, and thy sons, and thy daughters, and whomsoever thou hast in the city, bring them out of the place.
13 For we will destroy this place, because the cry of them is waxed great before Jehovah. And Jehovah hath sent us to destroy it.
24 Then Jehovah rained upon Sodom and upon Gomorrah brimstone and fire from Jehovah out of heaven.
ASV

God desires for us to have children only when we are married. It is only a man that can be a Dad and it is only a woman that can be a Mom. Only a Woman has the ability to be pregnant and carry a baby. Men have no wombs. Only women have wombs. No man has

the ability to be pregnant and give birth to children.
You should not become a Dad and a Mom unless you have finished College, have a job, and are married.
Before you can become a Dad and a Mom, you must go to School, be attentive to your teachers as they teach, do your assignments, pass your exams very well and get good grades.
You must go to Elementary School, go to Middle School, go to High School, go to College to study a very good Profession or Course that has the potential to get you a good job, and you must graduate with high Grades so you will stand out and have better chances when the Employers are making their choices of those they want to employ.

After you graduate from College, you should go back to College some more to do a Masters Degree and also a Doctorate Degree. A Doctorate Degree is also called a Ph.D. It is better to finish with all the levels of your College Education as soon as you can
By this, I mean: earn a Bachelor's Degree (BA or BSC), and then a Master's Degree (MA or MSC), and then a Doctorate Degree (Ph.D). You can get a full-time professional job while doing a Master's Degree and a Ph.D.
And you can do so at the same time as work and earn a good income while you go to School. Your Company will be glad to sponsor you and pay for it. With it, you will earn more promotion at your job and also earn more pay.

After a Ph.D, anything else you go back to School to do is additional and it is optional. It is not compulsory.
It is important that you work hard and work consistently hard to get great grades out of College.
This is to give you a quality chance in the job market when you are done with College.
By College, I mean the University.

I Pray

If you get great grades in school, you will go to a great College.
If you go to a great College, you will get a great job.
If you go to a great College, have much Wisdom and keep great Company and Valuable friends, the tendency is that amongst the circle of these great people you move around with and in, will be a special young man or a special young woman for you who will want to be closer to you than anyone else and want to marry you and live with you forever.
Several of them will float around you.
You must be very wise and prayerful to choose the one that is the very best for you.
Prayerfully choose the one that has the qualities that will make you happy forever.
Choose the one that you will always be happy and proud to call yours.
Choose the one that has the ability and the means to take very good care of you.
By ability, I mean his values and his behavior and temperament
By means, I mean he must be employed with a great pay.
He must earn an income that can pay the Bills, feed you, pay tuition, give you a home, have a car, and still have the ability to save some for any incidentals.

You will marry well, live in a great house, have great children, drive great cars, eat great food, go on great vacations.
If you get a great job, you will be paid plenty of money.
If you learn very well in School and in College and get great Grades, you will have great ideas to know what is happening in the world and what people need.
If you know the problems that people have and know what people need, you will have great ideas about how to help solve people's problems or provide solutions.

If you have great ideas, your ideas will make plenty of money for you.

In order for you to have great ideas, you must love to read and be knowledgeable, and you must always pray and ask God to give you Wisdom.

In order to have a great life, you must pray always.

When you pray, you pray to God.

When you pray to God, you must always pray to God with the name of Jesus and in the name of Jesus.

And for everything that you want to do, always ask the Holy Spirit to help you all the time.

Never underestimate the power of the Holy Spirit.

There is no matter or issue that is too high or too unimportant for the Holy Spirit to deal with.

He is interested in everything that concerns you.

God, Jesus Christ and the Holy Spirit are One and they are the same.

And so in everything that you do, you must make sure that you pray to GOD the FATHER. Pray to GOD the SON and pray to GOD the HOLY SPIRIT always.

And serve only God.

By this, I mean:

I Pray

There is only One God

And you must serve Him alone.

God has many names.
One of God's names is JEHOVAH.
Any god that is not called JEHOVAH, is not GOD!
Any god that One of His names is not JEHOVAH, is not GOD!!
Any god that is not God the Father, God the Son, and God the Holy Spirit, is not God!!!
Any god that does not have JESUS CHRIST as His Son, is not GOD!!!!!!

SOME OF THE NAMES OF GOD AND THEIR MEANINGS

Jehovah Jireh *(Our Provider)*
Jehovah El-Shaddai *(Our All-Sufficient God)*
Jehovah Elyon *(Most High God)*
Jehovah Shalom *(Our Peace)*
Jehovah Eloheenu *(Our God)*
Jehovah Rohi *(Our Shepherd)*
Jehovah Tsidkenu *(Our Righteousness)*
Jehovah Rapha *(Our Healer)*
Jehovah Sabaoth *(The Lord of Host)*
Jehovah Shammah *(Ever-Present God)*
Jehovah Nisi *(Our Banner)*
Jehovah Elohim *(Our Eternal Creator)*
Jehovah Eloheka *(Your God)*
Jehovah Hoseenu *(Our Maker)*
Jehovah Adonai *(Our Master)*
Jehovah Mekaddishkem *(Our Sanctifier)*

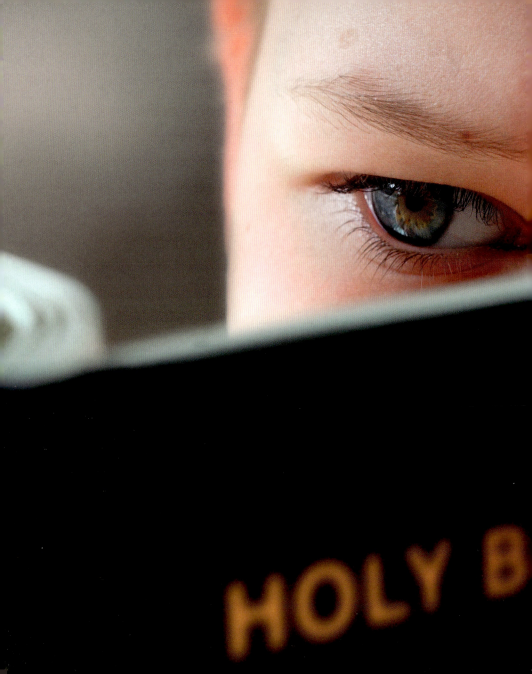

READ YOUR BIBLE AND PRAY

Always do 2 things:
1. Read our Bibles
2. Pray

You need God in order to be able to do everything.
You must continually pray in the name of Jesus. When you pray in the name of Jesus, your prayers will be answered.

The Bible says Jesus Christ is the Way, the Truth and the Life and that no one can come to God except by Him

Scripture:
John 14:6
6 Jesus told him, "I am the way, the truth, and the life. No one can come to the Father except through me.
NLT

I Pray..

THE HOLY SPIRIT

The Holy Spirit is a Teacher too

You need the Holy Spirit to always help you to pray, teach you how to pray, and tell you the things you should say and how you should say them.

He can help you understand the things you are taught in School better.
He can also help you remember everything you learn so that you can use them to answer your questions in your Exams and in your Assignments.
When you read your books, the Holy Spirit can help you get great Grades.

Scripture:
John 14:26
26 But the Helper, the Holy Spirit, whom the Father will send in my name, he will teach you all things and bring to your remembrance all that I have said to you.
NKJV

I Pray

So, whenever you pray, always pray that the Holy Spirit should help you

When Mom and Dad are there, you need God, you need Jesus and you need the Holy Spirit

When Mom and Dad are not there, you need God, you need Jesus and you need the Holy Spirit

Mom and Dad need God, Jesus and the Holy Spirit too!

THE WORDS: PLEASE, SORRY AND THANK YOU

Always use your best manners.

You must always use the words: Please, Sorry and Thank You.

When you need something, it is important that you ask:
Can I have ……….. please?

If Mom says: If you did something wrong or you hurt someone
Be quick to say: *I am Sorry.*

When you are given anything or a good thing is done to you, always say: *"Thank you!"*

YOUR DRESS CODE

Whenever you put on your clothes, your pants must always sit firmly above your belly button or around your waist.

Girls and Ladies: Whenever you put on your tops, make sure no one can see your breasts from any part of your clothes either through your under arm area, the sides, through the top of your blouse, or see your skin down below by your pants; they must not be able to see your body around your belly button area or your under pants at all.

You must take a good bath everyday and brush your teeth excellently well.
Brush your teeth 1st thing when you wake up, and last thing before you go to bed.

You must brush every part of your teeth – inside and out.
You must brush your tongue very well.
Your tongue must be pink and clean; and not white or coated.
You must make sure you rinse out your mouth real good after every wash.
It is important that your breath is fresh
When you take a bath, you must take a bath excellently well.

I Pray

Wash every part of you real good.

Remember your under arms, and your lower body private areas. Make sure the hair on your head is very well groomed, combed, brushed, done nicely and beautiful.

Put on clean and freshly laundered clothes
Use Deodorants after a bath in your under arm

Your Shoes – air your feet when you are at home and allow your feet to breath. Wear clean socks every day. Do not repeat the same socks.
If you have sweaty or oily feet, always put on socks or some foot lining before you put on your shoes and it is necessary to wear fresh socks or lining every day. Do not repeat the same one.

Same as your underpants.
You must wear fresh underpants every day.
Do not repeat!

BAD HABITS

Gal. 5:24 *And they that are Christ's have crucified the flesh with the affections and lusts*

Romans 6:14 *For sin shall not have dominion over you, for you are not under law but under grace*

2 Corinthians 7:1 *Therefore, since these [great] promises are ours, beloved, let us cleanse ourselves from everything that contaminates and defiles body and spirit, and bring [our] consecration to completeness in the [reverential] fear of God.*

Leviticus 20:7 *Consecrate yourselves therefore, and be holy; for I am the Lord your God.*

Romans 9:16 *So then [God's gift] is not a question of human will and human effort, but of God's mercy. [It depends not on one's own willingness nor on his strenuous exertion as in running a race, but on God's having mercy on him.]*

I Pray

Pray and say:
Dear Lord:
You are the God who is present everywhere and at all times
There is nothing that is hidden from You
I commit all my ways and all my thoughts to You
Purify my thoughts and my ways
Sanctify my thoughts and my ways
Address every hidden aspect of me that is not pleasing to You
Those things that I do and think in secret that are not pleasing to you
I pray dear Lord that You will separate me from them so that I will not do them no more
Bless the thoughts that I think
Keep them pure by your Words and by the help of Your Holy Spirit.

Separate me from every bad Habit that grieves You
Give me the power to do away permanently with every bad habit that I have
May they not rule over me

I pray that sin will not have dominion over me
I pray that Christ will redeem me
I pray that Christ will purify me unto Himself
I pray that I will be God's own special Child
In Jesus mighty name.

My God is All-Powerful
All Power belong to God
God is the Source of all Power

Scripture:
2 Cor. 10:3-5 *For though we walk in the flesh, we do not war according to the flesh; for the weapons of our warfare are not carnal but mighty in God for pulling down strongholds, casting down imaginations and every high thing that exalts itself against the knowledge of God; bringing every thought into captivity to the obedience of Christ*

Rev. 12:11 *And they overcame him by the blood of the Lamb, and by the word of their testimony; and they loved not their lives unto death*

Pray and say:
Though I walk in the flesh, I do not war according to the flesh; for the weapons of my warfare are not carnal. The weapons of my warfare are mighty in God for the pulling down of strongholds, casting down imaginations and every high thing that exalts itself against the knowledge of God ; bringing every thought into the captivity to the obedience of Christ.
I pull down every stronghold, I cast down every imagination, I cast down every high thing that exalts itself against the knowledge of God; I bring every thought of my heart into captivity to the obedience of Christ.
I overcome by the blood of the Lamb.
I overcome by the Word of God.

I pray concerning my mind
I pray concerning my thoughts
I pray concerning my intents O Lord

Pray and say:
Phil. 4:8 *Whatsoever things are pure, whatsoever things are lovely, whatsoever things are of good report, whatever has virtue, and whatever*

I Pray

is praise worthy, I pray that I will always think on these things and that they will guide my thought patterns continually in Jesus mighty name.

Scripture:
Galatians 5:24 *And they that are Christ have crucified the flesh with the affections and lusts*

Romans 6:14 *For sin shall not have dominion over you, for you are not under law but under grace*

Titus 2:11-14 *For the grace of God that brings salvation has appeared to all men, teaching us that denying ungodliness and worldly lusts, we should live soberly, righteously, and godly in the present age looking for the blessed hope and glorious appearing of our great God and Savior Jesus Christ, who gave Himself for us, that He might redeem us from every lawless deed and purify for Himself, His own special people, zealous for good works*

Pray and say:
I belong to Christ.
Sin shall not have dominion over me
I am not under the law
I am under Grace
By the Grace of God that brings salvation to all men, and teaches us to depart from ungodliness and worldly lusts, I pray Lord that I will live soberly, righteously and godly in this present age, in the mighty name of Jesus.
I am redeemed from every lawless Deed and I declare that I am Pure. I am God's special Child and I am zealous for good works.

Scripture:
1 John 5:4-5 *For whatever is born of God overcomes the world. And this is the victory that has overcome the world – our faith. Who is he who overcomes the world, but he who believes that Jesus is the Son of God*

Pray and say:
I am of God.
I overcome the world.
I am a Child of God.

My Body is the Temple of God
The Holy Spirit dwells inside of me
I belong to God
I have been bought with a Price
That price is the Life of Jesus
That price is the Blood of Jesus
I glorify God in my Body and in my Spirit
Everything concerning my Body glorifies God
The Clothes that I put on will glorify God
The way I look will glorify God
The way I dress will glorify God
The way I comport myself will glorify God
The way I speak and the things I say will glorify God
The way I relate to people and to others will glorify God
People will see my life and know that I am a child of God

ACCOMPANY YOUR PRAYERS WITH ACTION

Take a bold step.

As you pray, accompany your Prayers with Action in the direct direction.

Take action that are proportionate to the prayers that you are praying.

As you pray concerning these bad habits, make sure you stop doing those things that are displeasing to God.

Stop doing those things that do not add value to your life.
If it is smoking, STOP.
If it is a perverse lifestyle, STOP.

Scripture:
James 2:26 *For as the body without the spirit is dead, so faith without works is dead also.*
NKJV

I Pray..

WITH GOD, NOTHING SHALL BE IMPOSSIBLE

This is the time for your own personal requests.

There might have been some things that you want to pray about, that have not been mentioned in this Book.
This is the time to begin to mention them to God and to pray to God about them.

Luke 1:37 says: *For with God nothing shall be impossible*

Philippians 4:13 says: *I can do all things through Christ who strengthens me*

Pray and say:
I serve a God with whom nothing shall be impossible
And so I commit everything that is bothering me right now into the hands of God.

Begin to list every Concern you have and begin to commit every concern to God.
And as you so do, declare and say:
"with God, nothing shall be impossible".

I Pray

Pray and say:
I serve a God who reigns in the Affairs of men
I serve a God who is a Rewarder of those who diligently seek Him
God reigns in all that concerns me
God reigns in every matter that I am committing to Him
As I seek God concerning every matter and issue in my life
As I pray to God concerning every matter that I am committing to Him now in private, God will reward me openly by answering my prayers in Jesus mighty name.
God is the one who sees in secret and He rewards openly.

God is the One who sees everything that we do when people are watching and He sees everything that we do even when no one is watching
God is always there. He is always present. That is why His name is the Jehovah Shammah.
Whatever we do in secret when nobody else is watching, whether good or bad, God sees, and He rewards openly.

Pray and say:
I choose to do the right things even when no one is watching and even when I am in a secret place.
I shall always be conscious of the presence of God in my life because God is ever present and He is always rewarding.
I choose to do good in the Secret and I choose to do good in the Open.
This is because, for each one, there is a reward.
I choose the Good Reward.

.... I Pray

GOD GAVE US GIFTS AND TALENTS

God wants you to reign as Leaders, Rulers, Presidents, and Queens. In order to do so, God gave us Gifts. God gave us Gifts and Talents

Pray and say:
Dear Lord, please help me to identify my gifts and my talents that You have put inside of me

Scripture:

1 Samuel 2:26 *The boy Samuel continued to grow in stature and in favor with the Lord and with men*

Pray and say:
I will grow in stature and in favor with God and with men
I will find favor with God
I will find favor with men
I will grow physically
I will grow spiritually

I Pray

I will listen to everything that I am taught in School by my teachers
And I will understand
And I will always remember
During exams, I will not forget anything
I will not cheat
I will answer all my questions and answer them correctly
I will finish on time
I will get excellent grades that will always move me to the next level in class
I will be an Honor roll student
I will go to College and I will graduate
I will always use my best manners whether anyone is around me
I will always use my best manners even when no one is around me
I am a child of God

....I Pray

ROLE MODELS

Role models are people that you like and admire.
They are People you want to be like, or people you want to look like in their behavior and people you want to live their lifestyle kind of life

Samuel grew up under Eli because his Mom wanted him to become a Prophet. Samuel looked up to Eli and whatever Eli told him to do was what he did. He was obedient to Eli.

1 Samuel 3:1 *The boy Samuel ministered before the Lord under Eli*

Pray and say:
I will minister before the Lord

Dear Jesus, I pray that my Role Models will be people who are in right standing with God and in Society.
I pray that I will capitalize on the Values that they bring and take advantage of the good that they have to offer
I pray they will be people who have great values, people who make great choices
I pray my Role Models will be exceedingly Great People.

I Pray

I pray that the people that I will like and admire, emulate and want to be like, will be people who have done very great things with their lives, in their schools, in the kind of work that they do, in the kind of husbands that they married, in the kind of wives that they married, in the kind of children that they have, in the kind of homes that they keep, in the kind of houses that they live in, in the way that they speak, in the kind of clothes that they wear, in the way they serve and worship God, in the way they honor their parents and in the way they honor and respect others

.... *I Pray*

SAFETY

cripture:

Read: **1 Samuel 3:2-10**

Psalms 91:11-12
11 For He shall give His angels charge over you,
To keep you in all your ways.
12 In their hands they shall bear you up,
Lest you dash your foot against a stone.
NKJV

Proverbs 3:6 *In all your ways acknowledge Him, And He shall direct your paths.*
NKJV

Pray and say:
I will always be at the right place at the right time;
I pray that God will always direct my footsteps

I Pray

I will never be where there is an earthquake
I will never be where there is an accident
I will never be where there is shooting
I will never be where there is killing
I will never be where there is trouble
God will hide me
God will tell His Angels that are assigned to my life to always guide me and watch over me and keep me safe

Samuel was about 7 years old when he heard the voice of God
This was because he was an obedient and good child

OBEDIENCE

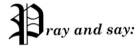

Pray and say:

I will have the ears of Samuel
I am an obedient Child
I obey my Daddy and my Mommy
I obey my Teachers
I will listen when they speak to me and I will answer when they call me. I will not mumble, I will not grumble, I will not complain.
My heart and my character will be prepared to swiftly answer when I also hear the voice of God and be able to know that it is God.

The voice of a stranger, I will not hear
The voice of a stranger, I will not hear
The voice of a stranger, I will not hear

HOUSEHOLD CHORES

1 Samuel 3:15 *Samuel laid down until morning and then opened the doors of the house of the Lord*

Samuel knew to always be where he was supposed to be. He was a good child. He did not imitate the behaviors of the children of Eli. Eli's children were Pastor's children but they were very bad children. They will not respect people who are older than them, they will not take turns, they will use bad words, they will not do housework, they will not listen to their parents, they will not say please, or sorry or thank you, they will not use their best manners.

Samuel laid down on his bed until morning and then he went to open the doors of the temple.

Samuel had morning duties. He had domestic chores and he did them. He made his bed when he woke up, he brushed his teeth, took a bath, put on his clothes, ate his food, cleaned up after himself, washed his plates and drinking cup, he always cleaned up his mess and always said thank you to anyone who made his food or did any good deed for him and also always said thank you to the Prophet Eli because Prophet Eli was the one taking care of him. He lived with Prophet Eli.

I Pray:

RELATIONSHIP WITH GOD

Samuel was afraid to tell Eli the vision.

There are some encounters that you have, and you get afraid to mention such encounters to your parents.

Never ever be afraid to mention anything to Mommy and Daddy. You must always feel free and comfortable to discuss and address any issues with Dad and Mom. Never discuss it 1st with anybody before Mommy or Daddy.

This is because Mommy and Daddy will always tell you the truth. And nobody will love you as much as Mommy and Daddy.

Scripture:

1 Samuel 3:19 *The Lord was with Samuel as he grew up, and he let none of his words fall to the ground*

This is Relationship.

I Pray

Pray and say:
Dear Lord:
May I have a healthy relationship with You
Make me Your friend
Speak to me always
Teach me how to know when You are the One speaking to me
Help me understand how You speak to me
Please help me to always obey You

Help me Lord to be a child of Honor and Integrity.
Dear Lord, please help me to see well, think well, and do well.
Dear God, please back me up in all of my ways, and let none of my words fall to the ground.
May the words that I speak be words of God.
May the thoughts that I think be the mind of God
Help me Lord to do the right things
I pray that everyone will recognize and attest to it that I am a Child of God and that my ways are ways of God and that I have the mind of God.

CONFIDENCE

The Story of Solomon
Solomon at the age of 13 was put in charge of a Kingdom. He was much too young for what he was given, yet he realized it and he also acknowledged it.

Scripture:

1 Kings 3:5-14
5 In Gibeon Jehovah appeared to Solomon in a dream by night; and God said, Ask what I shall give thee.

6 And Solomon said, Thou hast showed unto thy servant David my father great lovingkindness, according as he walked before thee in truth, and in righteousness, and in uprightness of heart with thee; and thou hast kept for him this great lovingkindness, that thou hast given him a son to sit on his throne, as it is this day.

7 And now, O Jehovah my God, thou hast made thy servant king instead of David my father: and I am but a little child; I know not how to go out or come in.

I Pray

8 And thy servant is in the midst of thy people which thou hast chosen, a great people, that cannot be numbered nor counted for multitude. 9 Give thy servant therefore an understanding heart to judge thy people, that I may discern between good and evil; for who is able to judge this thy great people?

10 And the speech pleased the Lord, that Solomon had asked this thing.

11 And God said unto him, Because thou hast asked this thing, and hast not asked for thyself long life, neither hast asked riches for thyself, nor hast asked the life of thine enemies, but hast asked for thyself understanding to discern justice;

12 behold, I have done according to thy word: lo, I have given thee a wise and an understanding heart; so that there hath been none like thee before thee, neither after thee shall any arise like unto thee.

13 And I have also given thee that which thou hast not asked, both riches and honor, so that there shall not be any among the kings like unto thee, all thy days.

14 And if thou wilt walk in my ways, to keep my statutes and my commandments, as thy father David did walk, then I will lengthen thy days.
ASV

Pray and say:
I have an understanding of who I am as a Child of my Daddy and my Mommy and I also have an understanding of who I am as a child of God.
I have an understanding of who I am in Christ.

I Pray

Dear Lord, I pray nobody will succeed in telling me anything that is different from what my Mommy and my Daddy are teaching me about God and about Life

I pray Lord that no one will be able to tell me evil or show me evil

May I never listen to them or be their friend

May bad people or people with wrong intentions ever be able to tell me who I am or who I should be or ought to be

May bad people never be able to tell or talk me into being like them or doing the bad stuff that they do

May no evil succeed in changing my identity

May I believe in myself .

I will have confidence in myself because I am an excellent child

I will not be timid and I will not be afraid

I will be bold

I will ask questions where and when I am supposed to ask questions about what I do not understand

WISDOM

Guess what? In this story of Solomon, God told Solomon to ask Him whatever he wants.

Solomon did not ask for a toy, he did not ask for money, he did not ask for a car. Solomon asked God to give him WISDOM. Do you know why? This is because, if he has Wisdom, then he will be able to get every other thing in the whole wide world – money, toys, cars, DS, DSI, WII, I-Touch, Ipad, and much more that have not even yet been invented.

Now, let us ask God for wisdom.

Scripture:
James 1:5 *Now if any of you lacks wisdom, let him ask God, who gives to all generously and without reproach; and it will be given to him.*
NKJV

Pray and say:
Dear Lord, the Bible says if anyone lacks Wisdom, they should ask of You because You will give generously and You will never chastise anyone who asks for Wisdom.
I ask for Wisdom dear Lord.

I Pray

I pray for:
Wisdom to live
Wisdom to grow
Wisdom to speak
Wisdom to think
Wisdom to do
Wisdom to accomplish
Wisdom to keep and retain that which I have accomplished
In the mighty name of Jesus

WILLING TO SHARE

The Story of the boy with 2 loaves of bread and 2 fishes
In this story, there was a little boy who was also sitting and listening to Jesus as Jesus was teaching. And then, all of a sudden, it was nightfall and everyone was hungry, but there was no food and there was nowhere to get food. But this little boy had only 5 loaves of bread and 2 fishes – his packed lunch that his Mom had given to him.
Now there were over 5,000 people listening to Jesus. They did not even count the children and the women that were there. And they were without food and they were hungry and it was getting to night time.
The Disciples went into the crowd to see if they could gather food and they saw this little boy who offered to give up his packed lunch! Jesus made a miracle out of his packed lunch and it fed everybody.

Scripture:

John 6:9-13
9 There is a boy here that hath five barley loaves, and two fishes; but what are these among so many?

I Pray ....

10 Then Jesus said: Make the men sit down. Now there was much grass in the place. The men therefore sat down, in number about five thousand.

11 And Jesus took the loaves: and when he had given thanks, he distributed to them that were set down. In like manner also of the fishes, as much as they would.

12 And when they were filled, he said to his disciples: Gather up the fragments that remain, lest they be lost.

13 They gathered up therefore, and filled twelve baskets with the fragments of the five barley loaves, which remained over and above to them that had eaten.
NKJV

Pray and say:
Dear Lord, may I be willing to share and give out of the abundance of what God has given to me.
Please Lord, always make a miracle out of what I have to give so that it can reach everyone who needs it so they will be satisfied and even have leftovers.

RELEVANCE

This passage tells us that there were 5,000 people without counting children and women.
Women and Children were not counted because they thought they were not relevant.

Pray and say:
Dear Lord, may I always be Relevant in the scheme of things that are good and not evil.

May I never be relegated to the background in the time of good in Jesus mighty name.

I Pray

RELATIONSHIP WITH MY BROTHERS AND MY SISTERS

Scripture:

Psalms 133
Behold, how good and how pleasant it is for brethren to dwell together in unity!

2 It is like the precious oil upon the head, that ran down upon the beard, even Aaron's beard; that came down upon the skirt of his garments;

3 Like the dew of Hermon, that cometh down upon the mountains of Zion: for there Jehovah commanded the blessing, even life for evermore.
ASV

The Story of Jacob and Esau

Genesis 25-27
Jacob and Esau were twins but they were always fighting and they were not friends.

I Pray ....

Pray and say:
Dear Jesus, may there be no sibling rivalry between me and my brothers and sisters.
May we be friends
May we look out for one another
May we be kind and merciful to one another
May we affect one another positively
May we dwell together in love and unity
May we never lead one another astray or deceive each other

The bible tells us that the devil is a thief and that the thief comes only to steal, to kill, and to destroy.

Scripture:
John 10:10 *The thief comes only in order to steal, kill and destroy; But Christ has come so that they may have life, life in its fullest measure.*

There are different ways a Thief comes.
The thief comes when no one is watching
The thief comes at night when people are sleeping
The thief comes when people are not aware
The thief comes when people are not looking
The thief comes when people are not paying any attention
The thief comes in our unguarded moments

And when the thief comes, it comes to steal, to kill and to destroy.

.... I Pray

What are the characteristics that are associated with the thief and the devil?
- Everything bad and evil
- Sickness
- Pain
- Disease
- Lack
- Curses
- Bad words
- Failure
- Hatred
- Crime
- Lies
- Disobedience
- Peer pressure
- Bad Habits

IDENTIFICATION OF PURPOSE

Samuel at an early age was told by his Mom that she asked God to give her Samuel and that if God gave her Samuel, she would give him back to God so he can serve God.
And so, Samuel knew the reason for his life.
He knew why he was born.
He knew he belonged to God because his Mom had promised God that she would give him back to God.
And so, at an early age, he was made to go and live with Prophet Eli so that he could understudy Prophet Eli because some day, he too would become a Prophet.

Pray and say:
Dear Jesus, please help me know, understand and identify early in life, the reason why you created me.

There are different stages of School I will need to go through as I grow up in order to get understanding.
In order to get understanding:
I must be focused.
I must not be distracted.
I must do the right thing at the right time.

I Pray

I pray Lord that I will be a focused Child.
I pray Lord that I will be an organized child
I must be a disciplined child
I pray Lord that I will not imitate or want to be like children who do not focus on their studies
I pray Lord that I will not imitate or want to be like children who do not do the right things
Dear Jesus, please give me a good character that will attract the presence of God in my life.

Scripture:
Ephesians 1:16-23 *I Cease not to give thanks for you, making mention of you in my prayers that the God of our Lord Jesus Christ the Father of glory may give unto you the spirit of wisdom and revelation in the knowledge of Him. The eyes of your understanding being enlightened that you may know what is the hope of his calling and what the riches of the glory of his inheritance in the saints, and what is the exceeding greatness of his power to us-ward who believe, according to the working of his mighty power which he wrought in Christ when he raised him from the dead and set him at his own right hand in the heavenly places far above all principality and power and might and dominion, and every name that is named not only in this world but also in that which is to come: and hath put all things under his feet and gave him to be the head over all things to the church which is his body, the fullness of him that filleth all in all*

Pray and say:
Dear Jesus: Give unto me, the spirit of wisdom and revelation. May the eyes of my understanding be enlightened. Help me to know my Purpose – the reason why you created me, and help me to walk in it. Help me to know what the riches of the glory of Your inheritance is as concerning me as Your child.

Please give me an understanding of the exceeding greatness of Your power and the working of Your mighty power which You wrought in Christ Jesus when You raised Him from the dead

THE ABILITY TO SOLVE PROBLEMS

Scripture:

1 Sam. Chapter 3:1-19
Vs. 19-20 *Samuel grew and the Lord was with him and let none of his words fall to the ground, and all Israel from Dan to Beersheba knew that Samuel had been established as a Prophet of the Lord*

Pray and say:
Dear Lord, please bless me with the Spirit of Solution
May I not cause problems
May I always have the ability and the wisdom to resolve problems and issues
When I speak, may I speak wisely
When I speak, may people listen and do that which I have spoken in Jesus mighty name.

PROTECTION

Scripture:

Psalms 125:2
*As the mountains surround Jerusalem,
so the Lord surrounds his people,
from this time forth and forevermore.*

Exodus19:4-5
4 'You have seen what I did to the Egyptians, and how I bore you on eagles' wings and brought you to Myself.
NKJV

Deuteronomy 33:27
The eternal God is your refuge, and his everlasting arms are under you.
NLT

Pray and say:
Dear Jesus, I pray that as the mountains surround Jerusalem, You will build a hedge of protection over and around me
I pray wherever I am, THE SAFETY OF God will be there perpetually

I Pray

I pray dear Lord that You will give Your angels charge over me in all of my ways
I will not stumble, and I will not fall
God will bear me up on Eagles' wings
Underneath me will be God's everlasting arms
In Jesus mighty name.

May I always be at the right place at the right time

Dear Lord, please be with me when I sleep and when I wake up
Please be with me when I go out and when I come in
Please be with me in my choice of friends
May I always hang out with only good people with excellent manners
I pray Lord that You will please keep me safe from all evil in Jesus mighty name.

CONTENTMENT

cripture:

Ex 20:12-17
"Honor your father and mother. Then you will live a long, full life in the land the Lord your God is giving you.
13 "You must not murder.
14 "You must not commit adultery.
15 "You must not steal.
16 "You must not testify falsely against your neighbor.
17 "You must not covet your neighbor's house. You must not covet your neighbor's wife, male or female servant, ox or donkey, or anything else that belongs to your neighbor."
NLT

These are the Commandments of God.

Pray and say:
I will be contented with what my Mom and Dad give me
I will be contented with what my Mom and Dad make available to me
I will never take what does not belong to me

I Pray

No matter how much I like it
I will never take what does not belong to me.
I will never touch or take anything that does not belong to me without the express permission of the Owner

I am a responsible Child
I am accountable
I am dependable
I am holy

.... *I Pray*

CHASTE CONVERSATIONS

Let your words and conversations be pure.

Scripture:

Proverbs 12:18 *There is that speaks like the piercings of a Sword; but the tongue of the Wise is health*

Proverbs 21:23 *Whoever keeps his mouth and his tongue keeps his soul from trouble*

Proverbs 18:21 *Death and life are in the power of the tongue; and they that love it shall eat the fruit thereof*

Proverbs 15:4 *A wholesome tongue is a tree of life; but perverseness therein is a breach of the spirit*

Isaiah 50:4 *The Lord God has given me the tongue of the learned, that I should know how to speak a word in season to him that is weary; he wakes morning by morning, he wakes my ear to hear as the learned*

I Pray

Philippians 4:8 *Whatsoever things are pure, whatsoever things are lovely, whatsoever things are of good report, if there be any virtue, and if there be any praise, think on these things.*

Pray and say:
I shall be clean in all my ways
I shall be clean in the words that I speak
The Holy Spirit directs my path
I commit the things that I hear, the things that I see, the things that I speak, the thoughts that I think and the things that I do, I commit them all into the hands of God.
Dear Holy Spirit, please take full and absolute charge of all my ways
May the mind of Christ be in me

Scripture:
Proverbs 4:20-23 *20 My son, attend to my words; incline thine ear unto my sayings. 21 Let them not depart from thine eyes; keep them in the midst of thine heart. 22 For they are life unto those that find them, and health to all their flesh. 23 Keep thy heart with all diligence; for out of it are the issues of life.*

Philippians 2:9-11 (Amplified Bible) *9Therefore [because He stooped so low] God has highly exalted Him and has [a]freely bestowed on Him the name that is above every name, 10That in (at) the name of Jesus every knee [b]should (must) bow, in heaven and on earth and under the earth, 11And every tongue [[c]frankly and openly] confess and acknowledge that Jesus Christ is Lord, to the glory of God the Father.*

Matthew 15:13 (Amplified Bible) *13He answered, Every plant which My heavenly Father has not planted will be torn up by the roots.*

Jeremiah 32:27 *Behold, I am the LORD, the God of all flesh: is there any thing too hard for me?*

Mark 10:27 *And Jesus looking upon them saith, With men it is impossible, but not with God: for with God all things are possible.*

Luke 1:37b *For with God nothing shall be impossible.*

Isaiah 54:17 *No weapon that is formed against thee shall prosper; and every tongue (lie of the enemy)that shall rise against thee in judgment thou shalt condemn. This is the heritage of the servants of the LORD, and their righteousness is of me, saith the LORD.*

Pray and say:
Dear Father, help me to incline my ears to Your Words as I read the Bible and go to Church. Help me to keep Your Words in the midst of my heart. Help me to hear Your voice. May I keep my heart with all diligence. May the issues of my life be consecrated and pure. May I live in Divine health from the crown of my head to the soles of my feet. I commit into Your hands dear Lord, every organ of my body, every cell, every tissue, every joint, every bone marrow, the blood and the water that flows in my body; I appropriate the power that is in the blood of Jesus over myself and all that is in me. I declare that Jesus Christ is my Lord. The blood of Jesus speaks for me. The blood of Jesus avails for me. I live in divine health.
Christ has borne all my grief

I Pray

He has carried my sorrows
Christ is the Price that was paid for all my Transgressions
Christ is the Price that was paid for all my Iniquities
Christ is the Price that was paid for me to have permanent Peace
Christ is the Price that was paid for me to have Divine Health
Christ is the Price that was paid for me to live in Divine Health,
Christ is the Price that was paid for me to enjoy Divine health
I owe no man in Jesus mighty name!
I owe no man in Jesus mighty name!!
I owe no man in Jesus mighty name!!!
God has given Jesus a name that is above every other name; That at the mention of the name of Jesus, every knee must bow, in heaven, and on earth, and under the earth; and every tongue confess and acknowledge that Jesus Christ is Lord to the glory of God the Father.
I prosper in my health in Jesus mighty name.
Every plant which my heavenly Father has not planted in my life, will be torn up by the roots in Jesus mighty name.
Dear Holy Ghost, come upon me in Jesus mighty name
Power of the Most High, overshadow me in Jesus mighty name
May I conceive and birth great and mighty ideas
May I be called a Child of God in Jesus mighty name

.... I Pray

YOUR BIRTHDAY

𝔖cripture:

Psalms 90:12 *So teach us to number our days, That we may gain a heart of wisdom.*
NKJV

Deuteronomy 33:25-27 *Your shoes shall be iron and brass; as your days, so shall your strength be*

Psalms 23:5-6 *You prepare a table before me in the presence of my enemies; You anoint my head with oil; My cup runs over; Surely, goodness and mercy shall follow me all the days of my life and I will dwell in the house of the Lord forever.*

Pray and say:
I thank you Lord for a brand new Year
Thank you for my Birthday
Thank you for giving me a brand new Year

I pray Lord that as I get older, may I get stronger, may I get better, and may I get wiser.

I Pray ....

Anoint my head with Your Oil of Gladness; let my cup run over with the fullness of Your joy and the fullness of Your Pleasures forever more
May Your Goodness and Your Mercy follow me all the days of my Life
May I spend the whole of my Life in Your Presence and in serving You Oh Lord

On this birthday, I pray for a special Gift from You Lord.
I pray for a Gift that is more than money.
I pray for that thing that is missing in my life right now, that cannot be bought with money.
That Gift that only You can give
Please give to me in Jesus mighty name.
I also pray for a Gift that money can buy.
Dear Lord, please touch the heart of my family and friends and everyone around me to reach out to me on my birthday to bless me with Gifts and with Love, and with plenty of laughter.
Make me feel Special
Make me feel loved
Make me feel Appreciated
Give me the Grace and the means to do the same for others on their birthdays too in Jesus mighty name. Amen.

BE MY COLLATERAL SECURITY

Scripture:

Isaiah 58:11 *The Lord will guide you continually, and satisfy your soul in drought, and strengthen your bones. You shall be like a watered garden, and like a spring of water, whose waters do not fail*

Pray and say:
Guide me continually Oh Lord.
Satisfy my soul in drought, and strengthen my bones.
May I be like a watered Garden
And may I be like a Spring of Water, whose waters do not fail

Dear Jehovah, be my Security
May I be confident of this very thing: That Jesus Christ is my Lord.

Scripture:
Psalm 24:7-10 *Lift up your heads O you gates, and be lifted up you everlasting doors and the King of Glory shall come in. Who is this King of Glory? The Lord strong and mighty, the Lord mighty in battle. Lift*

I Pray

up your heads O you gates; lift up you everlasting doors and the King of Glory shall come in. Who is this King of Glory? The Lord of Hosts, He is the King of Glory

Pray and say:
The Tuition for my education at every stage of my life will be taken care of and paid for
Before any need arises in my life, the Supply shall be waiting
I will not lack Employment
Employers shall favor me
I too shall become an Employer of Labor
I will honor my Parents
I will take care of my Parents in their old age
I will rise up and call my Parents blessed
My children too shall rise up to call me blessed

.... I Pray

PRAYER AS CONCERNING EVERY MILESTONE IN MY LIFE

cripture:

Isaiah 65:21-23 *They shall build houses and inhabit them; they shall plant vineyards and eat their fruit; they shall not build and another inhabit; they shall not plant and another eat; for as the days of a tree, so shall be the days of my people, and my elect shall long enjoy the work of their hands.*

Pray and say:
I shall build houses and I shall inhabit them; I shall plant vineyards and I shall eat their fruit; I shall not build for another to inhabit; I shall not plant for another to eat

As the days of a tree, so shall my days be

I shall long enjoy the work of my hands

I shall not sow and another reap
I shall not build, and another inhabit

I pray as concerning every milestone in my life:

I Pray

My Birthdays, my Studies, my Graduation(s), my Job(s) (after I have Graduated), my owning of Cars, my owning of Houses, my choice of who to marry, my Marriage, my Childbearing years and my Children, my children's growing up years, providing for my family, living a life that is better than that of my Parents, bringing them up my children better than I have been brought up, providing for them better than my Parents provided for me, my children's Weddings and the arrival of their own children, etc

Scripture:
Zechariah 4:9 *The hands of Zerubbabel have laid the foundation of this house; his hands shall also finish it;*

Proverbs 23:18 *For surely there is an end; and thine expectation shall not be cut off.*
KJV

Psalms 1:1-3
Blessed is the man
Who walks not in the counsel of the ungodly,
Nor stands in the path of sinners,
Nor sits in the seat of the scornful;
2 But his delight is in the law of the Lord,
And in His law he meditates day and night.
3 He shall be like a tree
Planted by the rivers of water,
That brings forth its fruit in its season,
Whose leaf also shall not wither;
And whatever he does shall prosper.
NKJV

Pray and say:
I shall be a Finisher
I shall finish strong.
My Dreams and my Vision will not be aborted
I shall fulfill the length of my days in Jesus mighty name.
I shall live to a ripe old age
Whatever good thing I start, I shall also complete it
God will bless the work of my hands

I shall be like a tree planted by the rivers of water, I shall bring forth my fruits in season, my leaves will not wither, and that whatsoever I lay my hands on shall prosper

I Pray..

GOD-CONSCIOUSNESS

I pray Lord that the Spirit of Prayer will be upon me
May I always be God-conscious
May I trust God continually and know that He is forever near me.

The bible says: Trust in the Lord with all your heart, and do not lean on your own understanding; in all your ways acknowledge Him and He shall direct your path

I pray that I will trust God with all my heart.
May I acknowledge God in all my ways
Help me to tell You everything about me and what I do and have been up to.
Help me not to hide anything from You.
As I do, may I feel You because You are real
Direct my path in all my ways.

May I always be God-conscious and may this God-consciousness make me very prayerful and always speak to God

MY PORTIONS

P*ray and say:*

I pray that my portions will be portions of Honor, portions of Increase, portions of Admiration, portions of Appreciation and portions of Value in Jesus mighty name.
I pray that I will always have more than enough

I Pray...

CHOICE OF FRIENDS AND ASSOCIATES

Scripture:

Proverbs 27:17 *As iron sharpens iron, so a man sharpens the countenance of his friend*

Pray and say:
I pray Lord for the ability and the wisdom to choose my friends wisely.
Help me Lord to be quick to identify outstanding, excellent and sterling qualities in people.
Help me Lord to identify outstanding and excellent qualities in the people I choose to make my friends and may they be friends who will affect and influence me right. May they be friends that will impact me positively
May they be friends who will be able to advance me and move me in the right direction in life
Help me Lord to be able to tell people apart in the words that they speak, in their way of thinking and in the things that they do
Help me Lord to be far from people who will deceive me and advise me wrongly
Help me Lord to be far from people who will take advantage of me

I Pray

Help me Lord not to trust people who are not trustworthy
Help me Lord not to tell all to those who will always hide value from me
Keep me from people who will always work against anything that is for my good
Give me Wisdom in Jesus mighty name
May the people I keep as friends be people whose values are better than mine so that I too can become a better person.
May those coming after me see me as a good example and Role Model.
May they aspire to be like me, as I aspire to be like those better than I am.
May I not be a disappointment in Jesus mighty name.

Scripture:
Isaiah 59:19
When the enemy comes in, like a flood,
The Spirit of the Lord will lift up a standard against him.
NKJV

Pray and say:
Raise up a standard for me Lord by the blood of the Lamb
Raise up a standard for me Lord by the Word of God
May I not be a disappointment to my Parents
May I not be a disappointment to my Gender
May I not be a disappointment to God

FAVOR

Scripture:

Proverbs 21:1 *The king's heart is in the hand of the Lord, as the rivers of water, He turns it wheresoever He will.*

Proverbs 11:27 *He that diligently seeks good procures favor; but he that seeks mischief, mischief shall come to him*

Pray and say:
I will diligently seek good
Favor will always be my portion in Jesus mighty name.
The Lord will surround me with favor like a Shield.
Mischief will never come near me
Mischief will never be my portion.
I am filled with the fullness of God
My God is able to do exceedingly, abundantly, above all that I can ever ask of Him, above all that I can ever think of Him or above all that I can ever imagine of Him
The Power of God is at work in me in Jesus mighty name.

I Pray..

Scripture:
Ephesians 3:19-20 *And to know the love of Christ, which passes knowledge, that you might be filled with all the fullness of God. Now unto Him that is able to do exceedingly abundantly above all that we ask or think according to the power that works in us*

.... *I Pray*

PROMOTION

cripture:

Psalms 113:5,7,8 *Who is like unto our God who dwells on high? He raises up the poor out of the dust, and lifts the needy out of the dunghill; that He may set him with princes, even with the princes of his people*

Pray and say:
My God is able to raise the poor out of the dust. He is able to lift the needy out of the dunghill.
God is able to set and the needy with the Princes
God is able to sit the poor and the needy with Princes.
You are my God.
Dear Lord, sit with Princes and sit me with Rulers
Endow me with Gifts and Talents
May my Gifts, my Talents and my Ideas make room for me
Cause Rulers to favor me in Jesus mighty name.

I CAN DO ALL THINGS THROUGH CHRIST

criptures:

Psalms 50:10-12
10 For all the animals of the forest are mine,
and I own the cattle on a thousand hills.
11 I know every bird on the mountains,
and all the animals of the field are mine.
12 If I were hungry, I would not tell you,
for all the world is mine and everything in it.
NLT

Psalms 75:6-7
6 For exaltation comes neither from the east
Nor from the west nor from the south.
7 But God is the Judge:
He puts down one,
And exalts another.
NKJV

Philippians 4:13 *I can do all things through Christ who strengthens me.* NKJV

I Pray

The Silver and the Gold belongs to God
The Cattle upon a thousand Hills belong to God
The Heavens and the Earth belongs to God
My God shall supply all my needs according to His riches in Glory by Christ Jesus

Philippians 4:13,19 *I can do all things through Christ which strenghteneth me …. But my God shall supply all my needs according to His riches in glory by Christ Jesus*

Galatians 6:17 *From henceforth, let no man trouble me; for I bear in my body the marks of the Lord Jesus*

Pray and say:
The blood of Jesus was shed on the Cross for my sake
I pray that the blood of Jesus will activate all the potentials and spiritual gifts within me in Jesus mighty name.
May the Grace and the Favor of God help me to maximize my potentials in Jesus mighty name.

May the anointing to Excel be upon my life in Jesus mighty name.

SENSE OF DIRECTION

cripture:

Proverbs 3:5 *Trust in the Lord with all your heart and lean not unto your own understanding. In all your ways acknowledge Him and He shall direct your paths*

Psalms 32:8 *I will instruct you and teach you in the way which you should go; I will guide you with my eyes.*

Ephesians 1:17 *That the God of our Lord Jesus Christ, the Father of Glory, may give you the spirit of wisdom and revelation in the knowledge of Him*

Colosians 1:9 *For this reason we also, since the day we heard it, do not cease to pray for you, to ask that you may be filled with the knowledge of His Will in all wisdom and spiritual understanding; that you may walk worthy of the Lord, fully pleasing to Him, being fruitful in every good work, and increasing in the knowledge of God; strengthened with all might, according to His glorious power, for all patience and longsuffering with joy, giving thanks to the Father who has qualified us to be partakers of the inheritance of the saints in the light*

I Pray

Jeremiah 33:3 *Call to Me, and I will answer you, and show you great and mighty things which you do not know*

Pray and say:
Help me Dear Lord to trust You completely
May I have a relationship with You
The kind of relationship that will seek to speak with You often, to tell You about the important things in my life and even the most unimportant things
This is because even the most unimportant things in my life matter to You
Instruct me and teach me in the way that I should go
Guide me with Your eyes Daddy
I am weak, but You are strong
I am foolish but You are All-Wise
Fill me with the knowledge of Your Will for my Life
Help me to walk worthy of You Lord
Help me to please You
May I be fruitful in every good work
Increase my knowledge of You
Strengthen me with Might according to Your glorious Power
Grant me Patience
Grant me Wisdom
I give You thanks continually and eternally Daddy for making me a Partaker of Your Inheritance
I thank You for making me a Child of Light
Thank You for being my Light

THE SPIRIT OF KNOWLEDGE AND UNDERSTANDING

Scriptures:

Isaiah 43:19 *Behold I will do a new thing; now it shall spring forth; shall you not know it? I will even make a way in the wilderness and rivers in the desert*

Psalms 119:9 *I have more understanding than all my teachers: for Your testimonies are my meditation*

1 Kings 3:12 *Behold I have done according to your words: lo I have given you a wise and an understanding heart, so that there was none like you before you, neither after you shall any arise like you*

Exodus 11:3 *And the Lord gave the people favor in the sight of the Egyptians (i.e. their masters). Moreover, the man Moses was very great in the land of Egypt, in the sight of Pharoah's servants, and in the sight of the people*

Psalms. 138:8 *The Lord will perfect that which concerns me;*

I Pray

Daniel 1:17-20
As for these 4 young men, God gave them knowledge and skill in all Literature and Wisdom; and Daniel had understanding in all Visions and Dreams. Now, at the end of the days when the King had said that they should be brought in, the chief of the Eunuchs brought them in before Nebuchadnezzer. The King interviewed them, and among them all, none was found like Daniel, Hananiah, Mishael and Azariah; therefore they served before the King. And in all matters of wisdom and understanding about which the king examined them, he found them 10 times better than all the magicians and astrologers who were in all his realm.

Exodus 31: 2-3
See, I have called by name, Bezalel, the son of Uri, the son of Hur, the tribe of Judah; and I have filled him with the Spirit of God, in wisdom, in understanding, in knowledge, and in all manner of workmanship

Pray and say:
Dear Father:
May the things You have done be my Meditation
May the things that You do continually be my meditation
I thank You for Your steadfast Love
I thank You for Your Faithfulness
Do a new thing in my Life Oh Lord
Let Your newness spring forth daily in my Life
Make it obvious
May I have more understanding than all my Teachers

Give me a wise and an understanding heart so that there will be none like me and none after me
May I find favor with You and with man

.... *I Pray*

Make me very great in my Society and my Community and my Country
Give me Honor and Greatness in Service
Give me favor in the sight of those around me
May my name be mentioned among those who are very great, among those who are the very best and among the highly favored
I pray for knowledge and skill in Literature and Wisdom
I pray for understanding in all Visions and Dreams
Perfect all that concerns me in Jesus mighty name
May I be 10 times better than the very best in Jesus mighty name
Fill me with the Spirit of Excellence
Fill me with the Spirit of God
Fill me with Wisdom
Fill me with Understanding
Fill me with Knowledge
Endow me in all manner of profitable Workmanship
Dear Lord, please make me worthy of my labor
May I be rewarded and promoted and may I profit much in Jesus mighty name.

.... *I Pray*

BREAK EVERY EVIL FAMILY TREND AND PATTERN

Scripture:

Galatians 3:13-14 *Christ hath redeemed us from the curse of the law, being made a curse for us; for it is written, cursed is everyone that hangs on a tree; that the blessing of Abraham might come on the gentiles through Jesus Christ, that we might receive the promise of the Spirit through faith*

Hebrews 8:7-13 *For if the 1st covenant had been faultless, then should no place have been for the 2nd. For finding fault with them, he saith: behold, the days come, saith the Lord, when I will make a new Covenant with the house of Israel and with the house of Judah; not according to the covenant that I made with their fathers in the day when I took them out of the land of Egypt, because they continued not in my covenant, and I regarded them not, saith the Lord. For this is the Covenant that I will make with the house of Israel, after those days, saith the Lord; I will put my laws into their mind, and write them in their hearts, and I will be to them a God, and they shall be to me a people. And they shall not teach every man his neighbor, and every man his brother saying: Know the Lord; for all shall know me, from the least to the greatest. For I will be merciful to their*

I Pray ....

unrighteousness, and their sins and their iniquities will I remember no more. And I that, he saith, A new covenant, he hath made the 1st old; now that which decayeth and waxeth

Isaiah 28:14-19 *Wherefore hear the Word of the Lord ye scornful men that rule these people which is in Jerusalem; because ye have said, we have made a covenant with death, and with hell are we in agreement; when the overflowing scourge shall pass through, it shall not come unto us; for we have made lies our refuge, and under falsehood we have hid ourselves. Therefore thus saith the Lord God, Behold I lay in Zion for a foundation a Stone, a tried Stone, a precious Cornerstone, a sure Foundation; he that believeth shall not make haste. Judgment also will I lay to the line, and righteousness to the plummet; and the hail shall sweep away the refuge of lies, and the waters shall overflow the hiding place. And your covenant with death shall be disannulled, and your agreement with hell shall not stand; when the overflowing scourge shall pass through, then ye shall be trodden down by it. From the time that it goeth forth it shall take you; for morning by morning shall it pass over, by day and by night; and it shall be a vexation only to understand the report*
Isa. 10:27 And it shall come to pass in that day that the burden shall be taken away from off thy shoulder and his yoke from off thy neck, and the yoke shall be destroyed because of the anointing

Isaiah 62:2-4 *The Gentiles shall see your righteousness, and all kings your glory. You shall be called by a new name which the mouth of the Lord will name. You shall be a crown of glory in the hand of the Lord, and a royal diadem in the hand of your God. You shall no longer be termed forsaken, nor shall your land be termed Desolate but you shall be called Hephzibah (means my delight is in her – the name of Manasseh's mother) and your land Beulah (means married), for the Lord delights in you*

Genesis 17:5-6 *Neither shall your name anymore be called Abram, but your name shall be Abraham; for a father of many nations have I made you. And I will make you exceedingly fruitful and I will make nations of you and kings shall come out of you.*

Pray and say:

I sever myself from every evil trend, tendency, pattern, agreement or covenant.

I separate myself from any inherited problem, sickness, curse, disease, known and unknown to me from either my Father';s family or my mother's family.

As concerning me, I declare that trend, pattern and cycle is broken in Jesus mighty name.

I shall affect my Generation positively

People far and wide shall know of me for good things only

I shall excel

My excellence shall get the attention of those who matter to favor me

My excellence and my good will never go unnoticed by those who matter in Jesus mighty name

I will be promoted

I will be highly favored

I shall be called by a new name which the mouth of the Lord will name.

I shall be a crown of glory in the hand of the Lord

I shall be a royal diadem in the hand of my God

I shall not be termed forsaken,

My land shall not be termed Desolate

I shall never be forsaken

My land shall never be desolate in Jesus mighty name

My life will never be desolate in Jesus mighty name

God will delight in me

I Pray

I will be married
I will be joyful
My land will be highly favored
I will be exceedingly fruitful
In Jesus mighty name.

1 Chronicles 4:9-10 *And Jabez was more honorable than his brethren and his mother called his name Jabez saying because I bare him with sorrow. And Jabez called on the God of Israel saying, Oh that thou wouldest bless me indeed, and enlarge my coast, and that thine hand might be with me, and that thou wouldest keep me from evil, that it may not grieve me. And God granted him that which he requested.*

I shall be more honorable than my brethren
Bless me indeed
Enlarge my coast,
May Your Almighty hand might be with me
And keep me from evil, that it may not grieve me
In Jesus mighty name. Amen.

Scripture
2 Kings 2:19-22 *19 And the men of the city said unto Elisha, Behold, I pray thee, the situation of this city is pleasant, as my lord seeth: but the water is naught, and the ground barren. 20 And he said, Bring me a new cruse, and put salt therein. And they brought it to him. 21 And he went forth unto the spring of the waters, and cast the salt in there, and said, Thus saith the LORD, I have healed these waters; there shall not be from thence any more death or barren land. 22 So the waters were healed unto this day, according to the saying of Elisha which he spake*

Pray and say:
Jesus Christ is my Lord.
He became I curse so that I will no longer be under any curse from my Father's Lineage or from my Mother's lineage.
I appropriate the power that is in the blood of Jesus to the source and to the root of my lineage on every side of me.
I proclaim that the blood of Jesus begins to speak on my behalf continually
I proclaim that the blood of Jesus avails for me
I lift up over my life, the blood-stained banner of Jesus!
I declare:
The blood of Jesus is appropriated at the source and at the foundation of my being
The blood of Jesus is my very essence
It speaks to my Joy
It speaks to my excellent Health
It speaks to my Provision
It speaks to my Education
It speaks to my Promotion from one level of my life to another
It speaks to my Graduation
It speaks to my getting married and remaining happily married
It speaks to my having children and remaining joyful
It speaks to long life for me
It speaks to favor
It speaks to peace
It speaks to every area that I know of and areas that I do not know of
My God is the Jehovah Shammah

I Pray

Scripture:
Jeremiah 31:29-34

In those days they shall say no more, The fathers have eaten sour grapes, and the children's teeth are set on edge.

30 But every one shall die for his own iniquity: every man that eateth the sour grapes, his teeth shall be set on edge.

31 Behold, the days come, saith Jehovah, that I will make a new covenant with the house of Israel, and with the house of Judah:

32 not according to the covenant that I made with their fathers in the day that I took them by the hand to bring them out of the land of Egypt; which my covenant they brake, although I was a husband unto them, saith Jehovah.

33 But this is the covenant that I will make with the house of Israel after those days, saith Jehovah: I will put my law in their inward parts, and in their heart will I write it; and I will be their God, and they shall be my people:

34 and they shall teach no more every man his neighbor, and every man his brother, saying, Know Jehovah; for they shall all know me, from the least of them unto the greatest of them, saith Jehovah: for I will forgive their iniquity, and their sin will I remember no more.
ASV

Pray and say:
My teeth cannot be set on edge in Jesus mighty name because Jehovah is my Refuge.
I bear upon my body the marks of Christ
I cannot be troubled

I Pray

I am not for trouble
The Christ blood-stained axe is laid to the root of all that troubles me or have been set in place to trouble me
Every tree that my God has not planted, I uproot in Jesus mighty name
Any door that my God has not opened, I slam shut in Jesus mighty name
Any door that my God has not shut, I declare open in Jesus mighty name.
I declare every evil and ungodly covenant in my life and as concerning my life that has been entered into by anyone dead or alive on my behalf; I declare all such covenants broken in Jesus mighty name.
I declare all such covenants null, void and of no effect in Jesus mighty name.
Christ paid the price for me
I owe no one
I owe nothing in Jesus mighty name.
Great is my Peace!

....*I Pray*

WHEN FEELING UNWELL

cripture:

Ezekiel 16:6 *And when I passed by you and saw you polluted in your own blood, I said unto you when you were in your blood, Live; yea live; yea, I said unto you when you were in your blood: Live*

Joel 3:21 *For I will cleanse their blood that I have not cleansed; for the Lord dwelleth in Zion*

Matthew 15:13 *But He answered and said, every plant which my heavenly Father has not planted shall be uprooted*

Mark 11:23-24 *For verily I say unto you, that whosoever shall say to this mountain, be thou removed and be thou cast into the sea, and shall not doubt in his heart, but shall believe that those things which he hath said shall come to pass, he shall have whatsoever he said. Therefore I say unto you, what things soever you desire, when you pray, believe that you receive them, and you shall have them.*

Matthew 8:1-4 *When He was come down from the mountain, great multitudes followed Him. And behold there came a leper and*

I Pray

worshipped Him, saying: Lord, if thou wilt, thou canst make me clean. And Jesus put forth his hand and touched him saying: I will; be thou clean. And immediately, his leprosy was cleansed.

Isaiah 53:5 *But He was wounded for our transgressions, He was bruised for our iniquities; the chastisemexnt of our peace was upon Him; and with His stripes we are healed.*

Isaiah 58:8 *Then shall your light break forth as the morning, and your health shall spring forth speedily; ....*

Psalms 107:20 *He sent His Word and healed them, and delivered them from their destructions*

Psalms 103:3 *Who forgiveth all thine iniquities; who healeth all thy diseases*

Proverbs 3:5-8 *Trust in the Lord with all your heart, and lean not unto your own understanding. In all your ways acknowledge Him and He shall direct your paths. Be not wise in your own eyes; fear the Lord and depart from evil. It shall be health to your navel, and marrow to your bones.*

Proverbs 4:20-22 *My son, attend to my Words; incline your ear to my sayings: Let them not depart from your eyes; keep them in the midst of your heart. For they are life to those that find them, and health to all their flesh*

Malachi 4:2 *But unto you that fear my name shall the Sun of righteousness arise with healing in His wings, and ye shall go forth as calves in the stall*

Hebrews 4:12 *For the Word of God is quick and powerful, and sharper than any 2 edged sword, piercing even to the dividing asunder of soul and spirit, and of the joints and marrow, and is a discerner of the thoughts and the intents of the heart*

Isaiah 55:11 *So shall My Word be that goeth forth out of my mouth; it shall not return unto me void, but it shall accomplish that which I please, and it shall prosper in the thing whereto I sent it*

John 8:36 *If the Son therefore shall make you free, you shall be free indeed*

Ephesians 1:16-23 *I Cease not to give thanks for you, making mention of you in my prayers that the God of our Lord Jesus Christ the father of glory may give unto you the spirit of wisdom and revelation in the knowledge of Him. The eyes of your understanding being enlightened that you may know what is the hope of his calling and what the riches of the glory of his inheritance in the saints, and what is the exceeding greatness of his power to us-ward who believe, according to the working of his mighty power which he wrought in Christ when he raised him from the dead and set him at his own right hand in the heavenly places far above all principality and power and might and dominion, and every name that is named not only in this world but also in that which is to come: and hath put all things under his feet and gave him to be the head over all things to the church which is his body, the fullness of him that filleth all in all*

Pray and say:
Dear Father of Glory, give unto me the Spirit of Wisdom. Please give unto me, the Spirit of Revelation. Dear Father, help me to know you more and more.
May the eyes of my understanding be enlightened.

I Pray

Help me dear Jesus to know the reason why you created me
Help me Lord to know my Purpose here on earth and help me walk in it to fulfill my Destiny in Jesus mighty name.
Help me dear Father to know the riches of the glory of Your inheritance
Help me to experience continually in my life, the exceeding greatness of your Power as Your Child.
Make me a living testimony of the working of Your mighty Power which You wrought in Christ Jesus when You raised Him from the dead and set Him at Your right hand above all Principality, above all power, above all might, above all dominion, and above every name that is named not only in this world but also in the world which is to come; and You put all things under the feet of Jesus and made Jesus head over all things.

Ephesians 3:14-21 *For this cause I bow my knees unto the Father of our Lord Jesus Christ, of whom the whole family in heaven and earth is named. That he would grant you according to the riches of his glory to be strengthened with might by his spirit in the inner man: that Christ may dwell in your hearts by faith; that you, being rooted and grounded in love, may be able to comprehend with all the saints what is the breadth, the length and depth and height and to know the love of Christ which passeth knowledge, that you might be filled with all the fullness of God. Now unto Him that is able to do exceedingly abundantly above all that we ask or think according to the power that worketh in us, unto Him be glory in the church by Christ Jesus throughout all ages, world without end. Amen.*

Pray and say:
Dear Lord
I bow my knees unto You Father of our Lord Jesus Christ of whom the whole family in heaven and earth is named.

May I be strengthened with might by Your Spirit in my inner man
May Christ dwell in my heart
May I be rooted and grounded in Love
Help me Lord to comprehend and understand what is the breath, the length, the depth and the height
Help me Lord to know the love of Jesus Christ which passeth knowledge
Help me Lord to be filled with the fullness of God.
Unto You Most High who is able to do, exceedingly, abundantly, above all that I ask or think, according to the power that worketh in me
Unto You Most High be glory by Christ Jesus forever and ever. Amen.

Peace
Isaiah 54:13 *And all thy children shall be taught of the Lord and great shall be the peace of thy children*

Pray and say:
I am taught of the Lord
Great shall be my peace.

PRAYERS FOR MY FAMILY

Scriptures:

Deuteronomy 7:13-15 -13 *And he will love thee, and bless thee, and multiply thee: he will also bless the fruit of thy womb, and the fruit of thy land, thy corn, and thy wine, and thine oil, the increase of thy kine, and the flocks of thy sheep, in the land which he sware unto thy fathers to give thee. 14 Thou shalt be blessed above all people: there shall not be male or female barren among you, or among your cattle. 15 And the LORD will take away from thee all sickness, and will put none of the evil diseases of Egypt, which thou knowest, upon thee; but will lay them upon all them that hate thee.*

Pray and say:
Dear Father:
I pray Lord that you will love me, bless me and multiply me in Jesus mighty name.
Bless my children, bless the work of my hands.
Bless me on my job and in my business
Bless my ideas that will add value to man and the society
Prosper them and let them bring me promotion and favor in the eyes of those who matter in my life

I Pray

May I be blessed above all people
May I not be barren in my body in Jesus mighty name
May I not be barren in my education, my job, my business and in all that I do
May I be Fruitful and yield results in every sphere of my life.
Dear Jesus, take away from me all sickness.
May no evil diseases in the world today and that which is to come ever be upon me in Jesus mighty name.
May I live in divine health continually in Jesus' mighty name. Amen.

Psalms 128 *1 Blessed is every one that feareth the LORD; that walketh in his ways. 2 For thou shalt eat the labour of thine hands: happy shalt thou be, and it shall be well with thee. 5 The LORD shall bless thee out of Zion: and thou shalt see the good of Jerusalem all the days of thy life. 6 Yea, thou shalt see thy children's children, and peace upon Israel.*

Pray and say:
Dear Holy Spirit
You are my Helper and You are my Teacher
Help me to understand the Word of the Lord as it is written in the Bible and as it is spoken by Children of God who are noble and who tell only the Truth, children of God who have integrity and children of God who live Honorably and Holy
May I never be misled in Jesus mighty name
May I be obedient to the Word of God
May I walk in God's ways and never depart from them all the days of my life in Jesus mighty name.
May I highly esteem God in my life and in all my ways in Jesus mighty name.
May I reap the reward continually and speedily

I Pray

May I find joy
May it be well with me in Jesus mighty name
May God bless me out of Zion
May I continually see and reap the good of the land all the days of my life
Satisfy me with Long life Oh Lord
Keep me safe in my life, in my health, at School, at play, when I am out, when I am in, when I am asleep, when I am awake; in every aspect of my life, may I find Your safety in Jesus mighty name.
May I live long in excellent health and prosperity to bear my children and to see my children's children
May my peace be great in Jesus mighty name.

Psalms 127:3 *Lo, children are an heritage of the LORD: and the fruit of the womb is his reward.*

Psalms 127:5 *Happy is the man that hath his quiver full of them: they shall not be ashamed, but they shall speak with the enemies in the gate.*

Pray and say:
I am the Heritage of the Lord
I am His Reward
I bring my Parents unspeakable joy
I do not bring them shame
I do not bring them Sorrow
I am their Unspeakable Joy in Jesus mighty name
As concerning me, my Parents' heads shall not be bowed down low in Jesus mighty name
God is our Glory and He is the lifter of up our heads
In Jesus mighty name.

I Pray

Psalms 16:11 *You will show me the path of life: in Your presence is fullness of joy; at Your right hand there are pleasures for evermore.*

Pray and say:
Dear Holy Spirit, show me the path of Life
You are the Alpha and You are the Omega
You have been from the Beginning and You still are and You will always be
As I live life, I ask that You take the lead in my life and help me to follow in Jesus mighty name.
Help me to live in Spirit and in Truth
May Jesus Christ be my Way, my Truth and my Life
May I dwell in Your presence
May Your presence be to me a pillar of Cloud by day and a Pillar of Fire by night in the mighty name of Jesus
May I experience the fullness of joy and pleasures all the days of my Life in Jesus mighty name. Amen.

.... I Pray

TO BLESS YOUR FOOD

Scripture:

Exodus 23:25-26 *And ye shall serve the LORD your God, and he shall bless thy bread, and thy water; and I will take sickness away from the midst of thee. 25 And ye shall serve the LORD your God, and he shall bless thy bread, and thy water; and I will take sickness away from the midst of thee. 26 There shall nothing cast their young, nor be barren, in thy land: the number of thy days I will fulfill.*

Pray and say:
I thank You Lord for providing me with good food always
Thank You for this Food that is before me
Thank You for the Preparation
Thank you that I am not hungry
Thank you that I am not Naked
Thank you that I am not Homeless
Bless my Food
Bless my Drink
Take sickness and disease away from the midst of me
Nothing shall cast my young
I shall not be barren in any area of my life

I Pray

I shall fulfill the number of my days
In Jesus mighty name.

Pray and say:
Dear Lord, I pray for Love in my Family between my Dad, My Mom, my brothers and my sisters.
Show us the path of life
May we be united.

I pray for my Dad
Please give my Dad the Wisdom as the Head of our Home. May He continue to lead us in the way of Christ. Establish him in his rightful place as the High Priest of our Home. Bless him as he works hard and tirelessly to provide for us. Provide for him so that he can in turn provide for us. Bless his job and his business and his Ministry. Make Daddy our great Role Model. Please Lord, do not let 3rd parties' influence and interferance tear our family apart. Give Daddy wisdom to shield us and keep our home together in peace and unity. Help him to lead us aright so we can follow. Help him to do good and not evil. May he not be distracted. Help my Dad to know you more and more. May he love my Mom more and more. May he appreciate her dearly. Bless his health. Give him long life. May I not disappoint him. Help me to bring him joy in all my choices and in all that I do.

I pray for my Mom
Strengthen her in all that she does to take care of us her children.
Strengthen her in all that she does to take care of everyone else that comes our way
Be with her as she runs all our errands, for our School, for our Home, for Guests, for extended family members, for friends, for Church, takes instructions from Daddy, takes care of our needs, takes care

I Pray

of our home, provides for us, stands by our Dad, and all the work that she does and how she tries to joggle so many at the same time to take care of us and the home front.
Bless the work of her hands
May she reap the fruits of her labor
May her labor of love never be in vain
May Mom be loved and appreciated
Bless those who bless her
Bind her and my Dad together with a cord that cannot be broken
May their love for one another know no end
May my Mom continually appreciate my Dad
May she respect and honor my Dad continually in the way that will make him happy and fulfilled
Give her Wisdom
Bless her health
Give her long life
Let her live long to reap and enjoy the fruits of her labor
May no one take her place

Honor my Mom and Dad dear Lord
Show them mercy
Give them joy
Let them rejoice continually
Let my Parents say continually: The Lord be Magnified!
I bring my Parents before You dear Lord
Bless their Marriage
Hide their Marriage and our Family in You
Watch over us and bless us with abundant life

Make me their unspeakable Joy
May I bring them joy in my Education
May I bring them joy in my Associations

I Pray

May I bring them joy in the Choices that I make
May I bring them joy in my way of life
May I appreciate and honor them continually
May I live long and become a joyful parent of children too so that my parents can also be a part of my children's lives
May I out-live my parents
May my own children out-live me too

I bring my Sibling(s) before You.
My Brothers and my Sisters.
Breath upon them and all that concerns them.
Help us to dwell together in unity
Rid us of jealousy, contention and strife.
May we be agreed.
May we love one another.
May we support one another.
May we respect one another
May we fear the Lord and not grieve the Holy Spirit.
Beautify our lives individually and corporately
Promote and Prosper us individually and corporately
Anoint our heads with the oil
Let our cups run over
May Your goodness and Your Mercy follow us all the days of our lives
May we dwell in Your House forever

Put upon us the fragrance and the aroma of the field that the Lord has blessed

Bind our Family together. Make it strong. Stand between us and the enemy. Let the enemy be far away from us. Let sickness be far away from us. Let calamity be far away from us. Bless those who bless us.

Favor those who favor our righteous cause.
Provide for us. May we not lack anything good.
Provide food for us so that we will not be hungry
Provide clothes for us so that we will not be naked
Provide Shelter for us so that we will not be homeless
Help us to live to a ripe good old age
May we dwell in Your presence forever more and serve You in Jesus mighty name.

I WILL DO A NEW THING

criptures:

Isaiah 43:19 *Behold, I will do a new thing; now it shall spring forth; shall ye not know it? I will even make a way in the wilderness, and rivers in the desert.*

Numbers 23:19 *God is not a man, that he should lie; neither the son of man, that he should repent: hath he said, and shall he not do it? or hath he spoken, and shall he not make it good?*

Psalms 89:34 *My covenant will I not break, nor alter the thing that is gone out of my lips.*

Scriptures
Genesis 1:28 *And God blessed them, and God said unto them, Be fruitful, and multiply, and replenish the earth, and subdue it: and have dominion over the fish of the sea, and over the fowl of the air, and over every living thing that moveth upon the earth.*

Romans 8:14 (Amplified Bible) *14For all who are led by the Spirit of God are sons of God.*

I Pray

Pray and say:
In Jesus mighty name:
I am the work of God's hands
I am created in His image and after His likeness
God has blessed me
I am fruitful
I multiply
I replenish the earth and I subdue it
I have dominion over the fish of the sea, over the fowl of the air and over every living thing that moves upon the earth in Jesus mighty name.

I thank God.
God causes me to triumph in Christ Jesus
In my life and in every place I find myself in, and in whatever I do and say, it is evident that I know Christ
I am a Witness.
I am led by the Spirit of God
I am a Child of God.

Scriptures:
1 John 5:14 *And this is the confidence that we have in him, that, if we ask any thing according to his will, he heareth us: 15 And if we know that he hear us, whatsoever we ask, we know that we have the petitions that we desired of him.*

John 1:14 *And the Word was made flesh, and dwelt among us, (and we beheld his glory, the glory as of the only begotten of the Father,) full of grace and truth.*

2 Corinthians 2:14 *Now thanks be unto God, which always causeth us to triumph in Christ, and maketh manifest the savor of*

his knowledge by us in every place
Philippians 1:6 - Being confident of this very thing, that he which hath begun a good work in you will perform it until the day of Jesus Christ:

Luke 1:45
And blessed is she that believed: for there shall be a performance of those things which were told her from the Lord.

Pray and Say:
Thanks be unto God who causes me to Triumph
I have prayed the Word of God
I have prayed the Will of God
Every Word of God and every Promise of God as concerning my life shall be made manifest in my life and shall become a reality in Jesus mighty name.
The Word of God as concerning my life shall not return to God void.
It shall accomplish every bidding of God for my life
It shall manifest in my life time
I shall behold them all
They shall dwell with me
They shall dwell in me
They shall be full of Grace and Truth

I am confident that God who has begun a good work in my life, He will be able to complete it.

Thanks be to God!

About the Author

Omo Ghandi-Olaoye is the multi-talented wife of Pastor Ghandi Olaoye who is the Pastor of the RCCG Jesus House, DC, located in Silver Spring, Maryland.

An attorney by profession, she has been in ministry alongside her husband since 1992.

Pastor Omo is the Founder and Pastor in charge of the Jesus Women Ministries, a women's ministry that addresses pertinent women's issues from birth to old age, with a view to positively affecting these areas in line with the Word of God.

The Jesus Women Ministries is the women's ministry of the RCCG Jesus House, DC.

She has the call of God upon her life to preach good tidings and hope to the poor and the brokenhearted, proclaim liberty to the captives, as well as reach out to women of all ages with a vision to helping them live their full inheritance in Christ Jesus.

Pastor Omo loves and lives on the uncompromising Word of God. She relishes in praising God and proclaiming the Lordship of Jesus Christ. She is the Founder of the 24-Hours non-stop All Nations Praise-a-thon. This is the Annual Jesus House DC Praise Conference that is held 1st Saturday to 1st Sunday in June every Year. At this Conference, diverse Nations are arrayed and featured in an atmosphere of uninhibited High Praise and Intense Worship with different instruments of Praise, Renditions, Dance, Languages and many more.

She believes very strongly in the efficacy of prayer, and knows without an iota of doubt, that God answers prayers.

Her life is a continuous testimony of a woman living the overcoming Christian life.

To the glory of God, she is the joyful mother of Fehintolu and Toluni, the wonderful set of twin girls God blessed them with for her 40th birthday and after 11 years of marriage.